The Fragile Voice of Love

Adam and Anne Curle, 1983

The Fragile Voice of Love

Adam Curle

JON CARPENTER

Our books may be ordered from bookshops or (post free) from
Jon Carpenter Publishing, Alder House, Market Street, Charlbury,
England OX7 3PH

Credit card orders should be phoned or faxed to 01689 870437
or 01608 811969

First published in 2006 by
Jon Carpenter Publishing
Alder House, Market Street, Charlbury, Oxfordshire OX7 3PH
☎ 01608 811969

© Adam Curle 2006

The right of Adam Curle to be identified as author of this work has been asserted in accordance with the Copyright, Designs and Patents Act 1988

All rights reserved. No part of this publication may be reproduced, stored in a retrieval system or transmitted in any form or by any means electronic, mechanical, photocopying or otherwise without the prior permission in writing of the publisher

ISBN 0 9549727 4 0

Manufactured in the UK by LPPS Ltd, Wellingborough, Northants NN8 3PJ

Contents

Prologue — 1
Introduction — 4
Bright light — 5
Explanation — 7

BOGGLING MINDS — 10
    Emptiness
    The body
    More adventures in the void
    Cloudy self
    Different floors
    Approach to therapy meditation
    Growth
    Human relations
    Love

HOSTILITIES AND LOVE — 28
    Changing signs of the times
    The hurricane
    War
    The philosopher's views – and fate
    Black Cloud – captivity
    Casus belli
    Conflict Transformation
    Evil?

OTHER STATES, OTHER MINDS — 43
    Notes about places
    Ireland
    Nigeria
    South Africa (Apartheid)
    Chitral
    Zimbabwe

Sri Lanka
Osijek

GLOBAL RELATIONS　　　　　　　　　　　　　　　　　　　72
    Humans and the cosmos
    Globalization
    The principal highway to Mind
    Great illusion
    First is last
    Conclusion
    The power of love

POSTSCRIPT　　　　　　　　　　　　　　　　　　　　　　79

NOTES ON INTER-SPECIES PERMEABILITY　　　　　　　83

ABBREVIATED VERSION FOR READERS IN A HURRY　　86

Prologue

A considerable part of this short book deals with the conflict between two powerful forces, the Black Cloud and the Mind of the Universe, but for us, the inhabitants of the Planet Earth, it is crucially important. The Black Cloud is a sad but crazily potent product of the earth. It has a kind of autonomous existence, rather like a lunatic escaped from the asylum. I place my faith, however, in the elements of sanity which we all possess and are struggling to preserve with our own minds and in the mysteriously gentle guidance which I believe we may enjoy from the Mind of the Universe.

The Black Cloud

This compound of fear and misery is distilled and expelled by suffering humanity in the form of sad and muddled feelings. These negative states of mind spread throughout much of the population. Their sources have been the spate of horrors that sullied the last century – the Nazi concentration camps, the massacres in Rwanda and later the Congo area, Stalin's Gulags, the fire-bombing of Dresden, the Battle of the Somme, the destruction of Fallujah, Darfur massacres, suicide bombing worldwide, and areas of global oppression and depression. Few of these have failed to touch us; few of us have not, however indirectly, been implicated.

Such is humanity's distemper, more virulent now perhaps than then, or here than there, though always somewhere; but with the world's growing population (until global warming really strikes) more and more billions are suffering (or dying), either from poverty or affluence. And we must remember that these things, or their kind, are going on *Now*. Although more is being done by many good agencies and individuals, more and more of our fellow human beings are being damaged, by repetitions sexed up, as they say, of baneful practices – read any catalogue for new ones.

The Mind of the Universe

The religions of the Book (Christianity, Islam, Judaism) believe, with some divergences perhaps, in a God who, amongst other things, created the universe. This is in some ways a pleasant idea, but leads to what I feel to be absurdities. For example, some perfectly sensible people were said to have been upset that God did not prevent the recent tsunami from devastating so much of the south-east Asia coastline and killing so many people. It strikes me as so much more probable that this terrible happening was a sad global need to shift the tectonic plates, without which some worse calamity could have occurred.

In conversation with the Dalai Lama some years ago, he said that as a Buddhist he did not accept the concept of God, but felt that some force must have set the whole vast system into movement millions of years ago. This is a position I personally feel easy to accept. Richard Dawkins' insistence on some sort of chemical explanation strikes me as harder to believe (and that's really what it comes down to at this stage).

However, there is a considerable amount of communication (though recognizing without understanding) between heavenly bodies, particularly those which are part of a system, as we are of the solar system.

I approach the end of this part of an inconclusive discussion with the tentative suggestion that there may be some level of constructive communication between what we used to term nicely, heavenly bodies. It is perhaps not an excessive leap to suggest that these solar or other systems might communicate *in some form* with individuals.

And I would go further with this problematical hypothesis. If individuals feel this to be happening, communication with the Mind of the Universe could be mistaken for that with God. There would, I think, be a considerable difference between communication with the Mind of the Universe (a possibly misleading term), and that with 'God', but it would be more localized, less remote and essentially more credible (if one can so think of such enormous spaces). Possible direct experiences of the Mind of the Universe will be considered later in the book.

The human factor

All human beings have the privilege of potential perfection. That is to say, there is nothing inherent to prevent us from attaining sanctity. The spiritual, or psychic, *equipment* is there for us to use. We coo sentimentally over babies, sensing inarticulately that they are still unsullied, but fear that they won't remain so. And in fact a great number of individuals remain remarkably pure. But we are warned about what Buddhists call the three poisons or fires.

I find these fires realistically both warning and encouraging. There is an unquestionable threat, but the fact that there is an explicit and carefully defined danger implies there is a way of avoiding it – difficult and demanding, but not completely impossible.

There are three clusters of dangerous moral errors, conventionally arranged around a circle. At the apex usually is the symbol of a Cockerel standing for stupidity and gross ignorance, particularly concerning the mind. Next a Pig, representing gluttonous acquisition, being misled by the foolish Cockerel's vain promise of plentiful delights. In violent anger at this deception, the Pig invokes the third group of poisons – the Serpent's hatred, anger and violence, directed against the deceitful Cockerel, whose ignorant confusion is increased. Thus the wheel of anger, misery and desperation continues to go round and round and ...

It's an ugly sequence, but one alas we know too well. But knowing it well, we have a chance of not falling into these very traps of ignorance and its miseries.

The Human Factor has I believe an important part to play, at least in our small corner of the mighty welter of the heavens. The reason for my faith in our kind is this: we have the evidence of human lives which have exercised free will by resisting the cycle, thus growing stronger and wiser, and achieving great wonders of love and beauty in the process. The Mind of the Universe seems to be a powerful force, but perhaps not one offering much obvious scope for human initiative. The Black Cloud, admittedly, is much more 'man-made', but is a sadly inchoate mass-produced human creation that suggests little scope for human enterprise. Its only use is to dissolve, leaving place for greater growth.

Introduction

An earlier version of this Introduction asserted very firmly that it was not a religious piece of writing; there would be no attempt to interpret the Deity's role in human affairs, nor speculate on the divine purpose.

Subsequent events, however, induce me to define my purpose differently. I still do not intend to discuss or debate on any hypothetical relations between God and humanity. Moreover the happenings I refer to (which are described in the Postscript) have nothing to do with the doctrines, practices, creeds or tenets of any particular faith. I would only say, however, that they were conspicuously benign and otherworldly. If that definition makes them religious or even religions, so be it; if otherwise, I may serve to avoid the violent conflicts which some faiths seem to relish, perhaps as a means of 'spreading the light'.

Irrespective of this issue, and looking back on what I have written, I feel I have done scant justice to the magnificence of the creative forces reflected, so far as we know, in every corner of the endless universe. Nor do I mention the wonderful Jesus (whether, as some theologians would maintain, a myth, not a man). But I am writing about human beings (including, if desirable, their religion, but as a set of psychological postulates) rather than an intruding divinity with a teaching.

All in all, I am concerned with how we live, or love, or cope with the world of religious or political leaders – who are also of course human beings. Some are zealous to instruct or organize us. A handy motto for such persons might be: Preach about (what you mustn't do); order about (what you must). Some of these are, of course, splendid people, but others are driven by lust for power, by greed and by a sheer stupidity.

Others simply love and respect us. These are the true leaders of humanity, descendants in a direct spiritual line from one or other of the great teachers. They can be recognized by their amazing generosity in both giving and receiving unconditional love.

I should perhaps mention one other point about the rest of this short book. It does not contain, as do most books written by academics – including myself – footnotes or appendices. The reason is that I don't consider it necessary. I am not trying to prove anything, to show that one interpretation of a fact or an event or a theory is more correct than another. I am simply painting a picture of a scene I know well.

Bright light

Some time in late December 1937, when I was a very young man, I was travelling in the desert some distance west from the Nile. I was what might be termed the apprentice of an older and much more experienced man, later a knighted professor at Oxford. Some readers may be able to identify this exceptional person, to whom I owe a great deal.

With us were five Arabs and five camels, the latter carrying skins of water and sacks containing food, mainly for them. This, if I remember more or less rightly – it was long ago and I don't have any notes – and consisted of fodder for the animals, dried dates, and a kind of dried bread called (I think) *aish shamsi*. The Arabs had their own food which was much like ours, except for the sardines.

We started off going to a fairly large oasis, and thence off south intending to follow a chain of small oases, some minute and uninhabited, but we expected, as we had been told, to be able to replenish our supply of camel fodder as we went along. But we could not: there was just no fodder to be had.

The only thing to be done was to return to the Nile, now several days march to the east. Between us and the river was, however, a high plateau. The ascent was easy and gradual and we found a fine place to camp. Others had found it too; we saw a few signs of earlier campers – an archaic sardine tin (our maps showed no signs of recorded crossings) and crude carvings on a rough wall of stones, a wind break on which centuries ago travellers had recorded their visit. A strange desolate place; there were no insects even.

Next morning our troubles began. The descent from the plateau was quite different from the ascent. The men could scramble down, but not the camels. But without the camels there could not be enough water to get to the river. So we hopefully but anxiously stumbled round the edge of the plateau. One of the camels collapsed. We went on, but one of the Arabs stayed with it. After a while he caught up with us, along. 'Darabtu,' he said grimly, 'I polished him off.'

At last we found a feasible way for both humans and animals.

We walked for eighteen hours. No one talked much. My sandals had collapsed and as we approached the river the ground grew rougher, the stones sharper (or so I thought). We got lost in the maze of venomous little hills, the sort of place abounding in hyenas and scorpions. Odd little visions danced before my exhausted eyes. None of us knew how to get through the hills to the river.

Then suddenly, as we stumbled to the top of a little ridge, there was a light. 'Fanus, fanus,' cried the Arabs – the great light. My colleague said, 'Yes, there's always a searchlight at the Assuan dam. Just follow the fanus and we'll soon see it. This is the best possible spot for crossing the river.' (This was the old dam, the present set-up is quite different.)

No longer tired, thirsty and footsore, we strode quite cheerfully down the now friendly maze of little hills. And then suddenly, there was the dam.

And as soon as we could see just exactly where we were, the light went out.

When we got to the dam, we told the guards that the light had been a great help to us, a good guide.

'Oh, no,' they said. 'We don't have the light now because of trouble in Europe.'

But this was Christmas day, and we had been following a star in the east that lighted us to our destination.

The other tales I have told have all contained examples of confused and cluttered minds. This one is different. I don't mean that our minds were not devoid of agitation and illusion. But I wanted to give an example of something far beyond our normal vision.

Explanation

Some time ago I began to become very interested in how we develop as human beings. What were the forces which impinged upon us to make us the sort of beings that we are? There are of course plenty of options to choose from, depending on which creed we subscribe to, or which evolutionary theory. What most of us partially, or in some cases fervently, believe is some aspect of the Christian or indeed the Muslim creation story; namely that God has endowed an element of his being, the soul, to every human. This naturally has profound implications for our nature and hence behaviour. If we sin, we contravene God's (and Abraham's?) ordinance: the ten commandments are a fairly comprehensive collection of prohibitions. Play by the rule book and you are pretty safe except for the most esoteric aspects of salacity or moral depravity. But of course there are also creeds that tolerate and even encourage the most repellent sins, such as torture and murder, provided you belong to an extreme branch of a recognised branch of some much respected faith.

There is also, however, a very largely different approach to our spiritual composition among Buddhists and other related faiths such as Daoism and, I am told by a friend, many of the native African faiths. (The European former colonists of that continent tend to believe that what they refer to as 'African religion' is merely a simplified form of some Protestant sect, or Catholicism.)

The Buddhists and their semi-partners in faith believe neither in God nor, logically, the soul. With the theists they share crude but comparable ethical values, but they view the structure of the human psyche somewhat differently.

Buddhism does not believe in the soul, but in mind. This is the universal primordial essence which must be nurtured until it is liberated and merged with the universality of Mind. I dare to say that many Christians, and I believe most Muslims, work to improve and educate their minds, and humbly cultivate their spiritual essence to find favour with God.

To sum up crudely the difference of these two modes: the Christian-type interpretation of human nature is that our main task is to please God, who may then open up wider communications with the God-given soul. The Buddhist recognises no soul, but a liberated Mind, in fact state of *being*, the Void.

This touches on the issue of *Emptiness*, also a keynote of Meister Eckhart's faith (he is the only Christian mystic whom I shall mention; I do so because he shares the vision of virtually all mystics of whatever faith). Emptiness, which could also be called *Wholeness*, is a reality which includes all the great panoply of the universe, from the dance of the galaxy to the rhythm of the corpuscles in your veins and mine. Separate the one from the other, and neither exists; join them and the wholeness is completion. Separate them and they are of no use as salad dressing.

Much that we discuss as spiritual is no more a revelation than are the fish without chips, to continue my earlier analogy. Such talk does not give a taste of the divine, but only titillates an unhealthy fascination with 'mysteries' that have no true relevance to life.

Finally, I must explain a little more about the phenomenon, concept, or whatever is the right term, of the Black Cloud, which occurs on many of these pages. Essentially, it is like a nasty smell. It's there. We are unpleasantly aware of it, but we get accustomed to it. It can be defined as a kind of universal emanation of unhappiness, misery even, frustration, sense of loss and so on, which is seldom far away from us, Most of us are unaware of it most of the time. When we are sensitive to it we may just experience a vague or fugitive sense of depression or unease, a mental non-specific miasma, probably transient and to be ignored.

Some of the Black Cloud which I shall be referring to, however, is more serious and can be very damaging. It is the impact of the accumulated misery, despair, desperation forged by the century-long slaughter since the outbreak of World War II, a butchery unparalleled in human history. It is, I am sure, responsible not only for immeasurable grief, but for desperate, foolish and immensely cruel actions. Among others I would identify the Rwanda massacre and the related continuing slaughter in Burundi and the Western Congo. In these and in countless other cases (the Gujerat massacres of 2004, for example) stupidity and ignorance underlie, intensify and interact with the usual base of ignorance. No more horrible, but ultimately far more dangerous are the cumulative nuclear policies of powerful nations. Equally insane in many parts of the world is the disregard for the global importance of preserving the environment – I can't blame the operatives and craftsmen.

I really criticize my fear of the Black Cloud of which the reader will see so much unless s/he keeps eyes and mind shut. But that's no way to deal with it. It's there, it's destructive, but there are more lasting and powerful states of mind: the Black Cloud emerges from misery, fear and anger increasingly virulent.

We must always remember, however, that the Black Cloud is lodged in and expressed through the memories and emotions and the inherited traits of the men, women and, most sadly, the children of much of the world. In particular many of the vulnerable and receptive adolescents are sucked into an ambience of fear, anger, muddle and chaotic violence. There's little wonder that the young are deeply distressed and 'difficult'. Moreover, as time passes the different tragedies and miseries of the past blend confusingly with the afflictions of the present to challenge the skills of the most insightful therapist.

But Mind, the Mind of the Universe, of which we are all a part since it reaches into every cranny of the universe with its power, is an infinitely greater force than the Black Cloud, but it is like the distant thunder compared with a door slammed nearby to deafen and disturb us. This is not to say that the Black Cloud's rage is harmless. It can administer a vicious jab on the pride, kick up the peace of mind, or shatter self-satisfaction, but seldom forgive or forget.

By contrast the Mind of the Universe brings many things. What it delivers to the planets and other heavenly bodies (as they are called, but probably no more so than yours or mine) we really don't know except through largely incomprehensible radio waves. Of the Mind's gifts, my favourites are Love, Compassion, Courage, and Generosity. You can't have one without the other, though you can switch them around and gauge them differently.

But hang on to them, for your life if necessary. Because if you don't, the Black Cloud will sweep them away.

So above all, love, let's love and do it generously with a full heart; and be deeply sorry for those who find loving hard; and if you do, be courageous to face the difficulties on the way. And spare an affectionate thought for the poor Black Cloud; its displeasing ways are the products of its pains.

My fundamental theme, from this start to the end, is: 'Love Lovers'.

Boggling minds

Emptiness

My bedside telephone woke me at six. Thoughtfully, it hardly ever rings, leaving that menial job to one in the living room. Not being quite ready to wake up, I was slightly annoyed to be roused so early, but intrigued that anyone should have called me so betimes. Then it stopped. It did, however, leave a message for my mind, though not in my ear. Why not write something about life as a human being in this period. 'Why not?' I thought, and mentally thanked whoever had sent the message.

I start with the central theme of everything that follows: the concept of Emptiness. The simplest and briefest analysis is that of the great fourteenth-century mystic, Meister Eckhart, who in a statement refuting the charge of heresy wrote, 'A man should be empty of self and all things'.

A much more elaborate, but completely consistent, assay comprises the famous Heart Sutra of the Buddha.

Essentially it says that nothing, not a person, a bodily organ, an object, an idea, a nation, exists as a thing in itself. Individual human beings may feel themselves to be unique, separate beings, but even the idea of believing this is produced by a complex interplay of heredity and a variety of current circumstances. There is no *wholeness*, such as one might assume a table to have; or as a table might be. Turning this around, it is quite apparent that a table is not an entirety: what about the legs? Equally, the legs are not the table. In the same way John is not a unity: would he be as he seems to be, without his parents, his wife, his children, his colleagues, the people he dislikes? He may feel he is, but in different circumstances – if he is drunk, in love, frightened, happy, sad – a different John emerges. Who is John? He is the product of an almost infinite number of forces – cultural, genetic, educational, social, etc., etc. *ad infinitum*. From time to time he is affected by a rather unusual combination of factors: 'John isn't himself today,' we say to each other. Or, 'You wouldn't know John, he's *quite a different person today.*' Significantly, the word 'person' comes from the Latin for mask.

Most contemporary psychologists don't approach the issue of identity in the same way. They are more concerned with the problems of therapy, which are largely to do with issues of the relations between the different 'persons' in the same man or woman.

But who is the real self? Do we have real selves apart from 'personae'?

The answer is that we can make one, or perhaps rather that we can *be, and in fact are ARE, a part of one.*

Most of these ideas contravene the aim and perhaps the moral principles of modern psychotherapy, of the 'popular' psychology of weak and strong personalities, of quirks and types, and of peculiarities. I am not suggesting that such 'types' do not exist. But they have nothing to do with what Eckhart is referring to. Not for him the mind which is chock full of fantasies, of paranoia, or neurosis in general, or for that matter, the intricacies of social or theological debate. No, anything that closes the mind or diverts it from receptivity, simply contaminates it. Indeed, Meister Eckhart's spiritual sensitivity, as opposed to theological orthodoxy, is shown by his approving references to Avicenna, the Arab philosopher and physician.

Many minds are preoccupied with speculations, fears, fancies and passions. But however brilliant and original these may be, if they are clogged with trivia, they simply obstruct the proper fruition of the mind into more complete awareness, more creative 'disinterest'. Thus people may dare to suggest that the genuinely emptying mind may be the staging post between the mind of God (wherever and whatever that may be) and that of humanity.

God has not been previously mentioned and the name will hardly be used again, but it is important in this sort of work to clarify the meaning of terms commonly employed. The Dalai Lama, while not believing in the 'conventional' view of God, felt it only reasonable to believe in a controlling force or forces in the firmament.

This is a viewpoint that I humbly share. It is completely beyond my belief that any architect of this gigantic system, so large that it takes millions of light years to travel from the outer limits to us, can be concerned with our little goings on. I also think it possible that at various stages in the development of the countless worlds, beings have evolved able to help existing creatures (presumably humans in the case of our planet). I imagine that in the case of humankind our early helpers would be some of those mentioned in Indian folklore and – within historical time – the Buddha, Jesus and later Muhammad, and in this epoch, Mahatma Gandhi, Nelson Mandela and the Dalai Lama himself, and between these stages, perhaps George Fox. The hallmark of these great beings is their ability to impart wisdom and peace to their followers.

If it is necessary for me to mention what we term God, meaning the whole of creation, I shall simply say Universe. This does not have such confusing names as The Almighty, which I shall not use (except by habit or mistake!).

It is of course true that the idea of our Great Creator inspires and encourages very many for whom the arguments in which I have been indulging are meaningless. For example, wonderfully spiritual music powered from the great Johann Sebastian Bach, who praised his God through such sublime music as the St

Matthew Passion, evoking without theological quibble its profound spirituality. (Incidentally, Bach was fined and then actually imprisoned by the elders of the church, who accused him of composing such sublime music that it distracted the worshippers from their devotions!) Not so some of the music of Wagner which evokes – very effectively – feelings of excitement and violence. The same may be said of some specifically military music composed and performed to enhance a spirit of defiant exuberance. This includes a hymn – not by Wagner, but in his spirit – 'Onward Christian Soldiers / Marching as to War / With the Cross of Jesus / Going on Before!'. (I need hardly say that this image of Jesus, whom I greatly revere, differs considerably from mine.)

The ideas which are interwoven in this discussion necessitate (at least for me) a certain amount of hopping to and fro. A page or so back I was talking about minds. I must now revert to that topic having set the scene in which minds function, the spaces of the Universe.

I was mentioning the problems of minds, their confusion and being cluttered with false selves. But then I encouragingly said that it was possible for us to have a real mind, not a mask or *persona*. This is because our minds are linked with, indeed are part of, Mind, a limitless reality. We make the error of confusing 'clever' and mind. Mind means seeing reality: for example, reality is knowing we love someone. Cleverness may be thinking up selfish reasons for not loving.

Sadly, of course, you will also meet the legions of zombies, those immobilised by self-absorption, their life fraught with pain and anger that are unhappily infectious. But while the body persists there is still some hope. What happens after death I do not know. But for the others, saved (one might say) by love, we can still strive to climb the ladder higher and higher into limitless Mind.

A further quality of our minds is that they are permeable to a great variety of information, impulses and opportunities. These may come from other human beings, or in waves from other of the heavenly bodies or even perhaps from Masters of the Universe. This may sound fanciful or obscure, but when we recall how much we are influenced by the moon – the tides, moonlight, moods (remember lunacy and lunatics) we may expect other things from other sources. With training our sensitivities, the permeability and receptivity of the psychic casing of which we all have some, may well increase.

As I remarked in the Introduction, I intend to embark on a piece of writing which is not religious, because it is not about God in whom I don't believe, but may have implications for those who do. Nevertheless, I find myself, both stupidly and cravenly, starting on what may seem similar. It is foolish, because I am ill-fitted to attempt to debate theological issues.

So I shall just go ahead.

I know a considerable amount about human beings, having lived with and loved them as son, father, husband, grandfather, colleague and friend but not enemy for 89 years. A little bit longer and my perceptions might have blunted; a little bit shorter and I would know less than I do. I have also been a soldier and a professor, have lived and worked in many parts of the world and known a vast variety of wonderful women and men of whom many, being old like me (or unlike me), have already died.

It's very exciting to be with children, to watch what's developing and to wonder what's coming next. If one knows – or indeed *happens to be* – one of the parents, it's both fascinating and miraculous. The little girl or boy has all, or some, or none at all of the traits of the parents. From every point of view it's miraculous. I am particularly excited when a growing child, even a young adult, suddenly reveals clear characteristics of a parent or even grandparent. How does all this come about?

We know the answer of course: heredity: the genes appear and reappear in a most fascinating way. And then there are the qualities that Indians might call Karmic. What strange happening in the past brings about some startling matter in the present? It's all very mysteriously interesting.

It may well come about, however, that there seems to be nothing strange or unexpected about our children or those of our friends. But that doesn't make their growth and development any the less absorbing.

My personal unromantic and inaccurate description of a young person's development is of a skin containing all sorts of interesting and unexpected items. These obviously include all the conventional items of physiology as well as the more subtle mechanisms which affect feelings, mood, personality, interests, artistic and creative ability and an infinity of interests, traits and skills.

As these begin to emerge, all manner of interesting things start happening. The skin sac of potentials is sorting out its contents. The young people are deciding which combination of skills and interests they want to develop as their main field of mind or body. This may be very difficult, depending on available resources, degree of interest, cost, and so on.

The young person involved here was an ardent musician, a pianist, but who also wanted to live quietly in the country. The opposing interests were very hard in this case, because they *reflected entirely different personalities* within the same body.

The other case was not so hard. It involved opposing interests in academic subjects, classics and history, the main conflict being between the student and the university administration which for some reason would not allow the combination.

As most people will know, however, such conflicts are not the source of destructive action. I really quote these cases to illustrate very common phenomenon: the cohabitation of two persons, or more, in one. Most of us have the idea of an idealised, brilliant, very witty, or very intelligent, or very something we have a dream of being, person. S/he may never be fully actualised, but I have been in difficult or unusual situations where someone has quite unexpectedly – and as one might have thought, quite atypically – taken over. *The last person*, people say; *who would have thought it?*

We must now break away from our young and not so young women and men, to fill in two factors which will have major impacts on their lives. One is what we have come to refer to as the Black Cloud. The other is the Mind of the Universe.

The Black Cloud is the name being given to the atmosphere of depression and despair which, to remind us, has been *distilled* from the collective horror and beastliness particularly of the last hundred years (and of course to some extent earlier) during which more human beings have been killed in war, persecuted, victimised in concentration camps, tortured, brutalised in prison, driven from their homes, forced to abandon their children, than has ever happened before in the same period of time.

These things sadly have happened before, but the world's population has never been so large or offered so many victims to the monstrous murderers. The result has been a sort of psychic fog which has seeped into the emotional lungs of whole populations in many parts of the world. The main symptom seems to be a sort of vague depression, confusion and loss of confidence. Among young people it may also lead to extravagant or aimless violence. In general it has an unsettling and disturbing impact on society – one which is likely to exacerbate any disequilibrium generated by the Black Cloud, and indeed to be a part of it.

The Mind of the Universe is diametrically opposite. I believe that many deists would believe that there is just God's intelligence and that it is the medium, via various messengers and prophets, to convey his teachings and messages. Undoubtedly space is full of waves which can be received but not understood by us. (We can, of course, receive on a simpler scale the clearest possible messages from the moon: night and day, the seasons, etc.)

I am convinced, however, that the galaxies in their countless millions, 'dead' and 'alive', whatever the words mean in this context, have some sort of purpose and function. The Dalai Lama, as mentioned earlier, has said that he didn't believe in God, but that something must have set up the whole business, and then kept it going. By contrast, the Mind of the Universe is, my senses suggest, a more intimate and personal contact.

We now return to our young and to some older ones, currently at critical junctures of their lives – in a sense we all are. Many of us are smeared by the psychic muck of the Black Cloud, but we are doing our best to preserve the balance and good sense that we were born with.

We are doing our best to cope with what might be thought of as the conventional problems of youth (or old age), affected somewhat by the Black Cloud, though that may not be what we call it, or how we think of it. But what we do have, all of us, is our own mind which is part of the great mind. The more we can drag ourselves out of the mucky slime of the Black Cloud, the closer we come to the Mind of the Universe.

(Please excuse me if I interrupt. I am trying to do something very difficult: to explain mental circumstances by reference to a material one. When I mention 'slime' I am referring to the mental process which leads to confusing or cluttering of the mind. This would retard its development of contact and eventual union with the Great and effective Mind of the Universe. The present danger of this is that the Black Cloud slime is sticky, rendering the mind clotted, static and stuck to its fellows – its worries, peculiarities, phobias, prejudices, etc. In this way its contact with its source of strength, the wider and more open power of the Great or Universal Mind, is diminished.)

And at this stage we must strive to open the mind, *our* Mind, to Emptiness. Up to this time, however much we may have recognised the existence of a vaster reality beyond, we have dwelt within the (now uncertain) world of mixed speculation and confusion. The *Self*, mine and yours, is shaky. Its glimpse of *Emptiness*, and its astronomic size and its wonder, are *devastating* until we make the leap of acceptance – and that may last a long period of quivering at the end of the diving board. When we have taken the plunge, however, we feel an enormous safety: we have dived into the security of certainty.

There is nothing to be afraid of, no lurking wolves of doubt, no trembling self.

Meister Eckhart was right. Safety lay in discarding the Self. But it's not ever easy. Little slivers of self stick anxiously around us, watching for a moment of doubt.

But why, you may ask, is Emptiness so secure? The answer is very clear: Emptiness is Wholeness. The Mind of the Universe has no subversive Self: it simply IS, unsullied by any hot whiff of confusion, greed or uncertainty. These have been left behind with the little minds with their clogging and confusion, but they have done a good job. They launched the projectile of mind, and will follow in due course.

The last pages aimed to give a high-velocity impression of an approach to viewing the position of us humans in the cosmos. In the following pages we will consider more particular aspects of our existence. I shall start with what I call a crowd of dead sheep. Why did I choose this unprepossessing title? Why indeed. Well, because I had been thinking about human failures to take full advantage of the amazing potentialities with which we are endowed. And I use the word 'failure', thinking of myself and others, let alone the collective hash we have made of our world, knowing that some of us, perhaps the majority, have contributed to such horrors. That is what I hope we shall be brave enough to discuss in the following pages.

Much that we discuss is no more the fruit of the spirit than condiments which add flavour but little nourishment to the boring food we eat. It is no more a revelation of reality than a psychic trick. They give no taste of the divine, but only titillate an unhealthy interest in 'mysteries' that have no relevance to the really enigmatic 'mysteries' of life.

What really matters is the relationship of one (human) being to another. To start with we have to realise the idea that you or I is *not* a complex, unified entity.

It is in fact a very complex composite, in which are a large number of factors (many themselves complex composites). But each of us has a temporary leader, which we call and think of as 'I', though it may be disposed of in times of shifting conditions (inner or outer, if these can be separated). A change of leadership brings about a change of the pattern of being.

The great question we have to ask is this: How can we, with our limited minds, free ourselves from the bonds of ignorance, and develop and/or preserve the understanding which could liberate us? Is this not like asking a legless man to walk? Yet some, like the great Masters, and some much humbler, have achieved these impossibilities. There are indeed many more – mostly modest – women and men who, in sickness, pain, in prison, in disgrace, have overcome pain and grief to comfort others. The Nelson Mandelas are a great example and inspiration; so are the long-suffering courage and good heart of the many (whether technically innocent or not) who generate the healing hope and love.

To the extent that we come to terms with these ideas, we feel free (rather than know, which is uncertain). We learn through our existence, through our connection with others, through shared love and grief. This is the reason why *solitary confinement* is so shattering: the essential web of interconnection has been largely broken. Equally, of course, it is terrible for any of us to be herded interminably together.

The subtleties and complexities of the Universe are obviously not to be plumbed through using larger and more sophisticated telescopes or more searching analyses of the soil chemistry of stars, but basically in our own minds. Here we need hard work to clear the obstruction of imperfect thinking. We need meditation exercises to free us from the prison of irrational thought and feeling.

Finally, it is needful to bear always in mind the principle of Emptiness. This has been constantly stressed. It is also crucially important to remember that we are assemblies rather than entities, but most of us, particularly the fruits of Western civilization, profoundly believe that we are *whole Beings*. I think, unless I am shown otherwise, that *I AM* a complete unit, a totality, a self-consistent self-contained entity, a *person* (forgetting that this means an actor, or with us, a bundle of actors). In fact we believe we are precisely what we are warned against thinking ourselves to be – a SELF.

However, it needs but a small step of remembrance to recall reality (that is, to *reactivate a slumbering mind*). Unless it is wide awake, it easily becomes open to self-satisfaction, worry, annoyance, anxious hope, fear, and all the rest. I don't necessarily means strong feelings, nor many, nor frequent, but to a considerable extent it is these small things that quietly clutter the mind, diverting it from its true quest, the wonders of Emptiness and the Universe.

The body

Many people who, like most of us, have bodies, may feel a little slighted that they don't get any recognition in these pages. There's just too much about celestial travel and such like, and not enough down-to-earth matters. Let me assure you, however, that bodies are just part and parcel of all the matters referred to here.

I too had often wondered what happened to the body when we die. Obviously, in normal circumstances it is buried or cremated or consigned to the waves, or something equally acceptable to the mourners. But is there no equivalent of the Black Cloud? Has it just spent x years as a convenient covering for all the personae which comprise the mind? Is it just discarded as we do a holdall after completing one journey and setting out on another?

I think not. The holdall body is simply a part of the multi-faceted life of Mary or John. We might just as well ask whether the lungs or liver would be disowned on death. The body is, so to speak, a functioning part of the being and all its other parts and energies. The actual spiritual physiology is, however, something we don't know about or have any need to.

More adventures in the void

Much that we keenly discuss as spiritual is no more the fruit of the spirit than learning to count is the essence of solving quadratic equations. It is not more a revelation of the inner self than table-turning or any other psychic trick. These do not give a taste of the divine, only stimulate an unhealthy interest in 'mysteries' that have no relevance in the real profundities of life.

We cannot sufficiently emphasise that what really matters is the relationship of one (human) being to another. To start with and as we often need to remind ourselves, you are a complex unified physical entity. It is in fact a very complex composite in which are a large number of such things. Each one has a temporary 'I' though it may be disposed of at any moment of shifting conditions (inner or outer if feasible) if there is a change of the pattern of being.

We all recognise, of course, that the psychic shell is permeable. Permeability varies according to circumstances. We may, for example, hear an interesting lecture which breaks through the shell and creates a change in the balance of the structure of the self (or ego, to use the conventional term). Or we may be in the vicinity of brilliant and creative people pulsating with energy, whose very presence stirs us, without awareness of its source. In addition, as with the concept of karma, permeability may be affected genetically, one way or another.

If we really understand the implications of this, we must recognise that 'you' and 'I' matter very little except as a temporary focal point in an unending system of life; no, of *Being*. Equally, to the extent that we are to some degree porous, we are open both to give and receive trillions of impulses. We are in fact elements of the creative force of the universe.

And what does that lead to?

Aspects of this are certainly manifested in our moods and feelings. No doubt strong feelings of elation, wonder, peacefulness originate in or are reinforced through mundane conditions.

One way of understanding this is selfishly insular, rejecting the universality of experience to which we are exposed. The other is to recognise that it is a tremendous boon.

The key to grasping the nature of this truly crucial potential is the concept of Emptiness. This overarching idea is that neither we human beings, nor something quite material – neither a computer, nor a star, nor an elephant – has a self. If I ask, 'Who am I, to which of my myriad selves do I answer?' the response must be: 'We,' and all other phenomena only exist in their relationships with all others.

After a while we give up efforts to understand all these issues at an intellectual level. Just accept that they are there. Our incomprehension is not something that can be resolved (except in certain respects by astronomers).

Paradoxically, however, the answer is not just a matter of larger and more efficient research laboratories. It is to some extent within our own minds – but always remembering that our mind (when our meditation exercises liberate it from the prison of material thinking) is also MIND – of which we are a facet, but cluttered.

We should then always remember the great waves of violence, the huge wars, the massacres, torture of the innocents. They arise like bodies writhing in torment out of cramped and mutilated minds. Clever men in universities, or the offices of serious policy makers, tell us that the source of the violence is in the economy, the social structure, the government system. But seldom do they blame the malfunctioning minds, the roots of violence tucked away under the mass of literary illusions. The mindsets of the two great wars, and many since, culminating in Iraq, should be enough to warn us against wars gestating in the minds of the powerful and callous.

Cloudy self

The Black Cloud and the concept of the self are intimately connected, but not identical. The Black Cloud, as I have tried to define it, is the collective tainting of the human mind by catastrophic and horrible happenings, such as war. Such are megadeaths, torturing, destruction of homes and communities, concentrations camps, massacres, brutal oppression that have dominated the world scene for almost a century. The misery and despair caused by these dreadful events have driven peace from the heart of many millions, even of those who have not suffered directly. It shows in distorted community life, especially among the young through violence and addictions and – naturally – hostility towards adults who, they feel, have so distorted the world. This is somewhat unfair because the Cloud affects them too, if differently. Take me, for example: I have not undergone the frightful pangs and anguish that so many have suffered, but simply knowing of these things and from time to time and place to place being directly touched by them, I have shared a fragment of the pain.

But the harm of the Black Cloud is not simply knowing about or suffering from these catastrophes: it *invades* the mind with illogical dread and unease and, in some cases, despair. In this way we share the misery of those who have directly suffered the imprisonment, the persecution, the loss.

One of the ills of the Black Cloud is that it distorts. We, who sit comfortably at home watching the television reports of war or famine, may well be relatively untouched, but the waves of terror and despair emanating from those happenings impart a deep uneasiness, the full force of which we may not recognize. The misery or grief may come from a past incident, but once a mind is touched by it, the reverberations will spread, perhaps very widely.

Belief in the self is an illusion, the ultimate illusion that 'I' is the Supreme Being – I love, I AM everything that is. The reality of Emptiness and Mind are utterly incompatible with that deluded self. They are also completely different, of course, from that of the ego. The ego is the self-concept which someone tries, not always with success, to present a favourable enough view of (and to) her/himself. Someone with what is called a strong ego is one who is self-confident, assured, holds strong opinions and expresses them emphatically. This is not the same as being egotistical, which usually means selfish but not necessarily strong-minded. These somewhat niggling little definitions are unfortunately needful if we are to identify the Black Cloud syndrome as something different from, if linked to, other emotional conditions, primarily perhaps anxiety, paranoia and depression.

I am not suggesting for a moment that the Black Cloud effect should supersede the existing psychiatric categories, but am simply saying that it intensifies and probably ramifies existing problems. It may also complicate them by multiplying the elements which compose them. For example, we do not know (as far as I am aware) whether different sources of suffering – a wound, torture, death of a baby from famine or from bombing – call for different treatments. There are probably many issues of this sort which have not been elucidated.

These uncertainties are probably ill-informed. So much the better if that is the case. Of one thing, however, I am quite certain. The physical ills to which so much of humanity has been subjected during the last hundred years have caused, or been amplified enormously by, misery. But at the same time we are also reminded that the self is the stumbling block, the shackle that holds us back from what we might do or be.

Let's try, however, to think (or imagine) about how we can overcome the stumbling block of the self. Or rather, having gone so far, ask what next.

To think back, we envisage that the hold of the self has weakened and that the power of the Universal Mind has strengthened proportionately. I can say no more. I can only feel sure that when (if?) I reach that point, the next tentative step will be a long stride. But whither?

I can, however, derive an analogy from the field of many human legal systems. These provide scales of punishment (so many units of currency or years in prison) for conviction of different crimes, allowing a certain measure of flexibility according to circumstances.

However, there is another principle of assessing punishment. This offers a different means of evaluating 'criminal' behaviour – mercy. For example, a physician may administer a lethal drug to a terminally ill patient in great pain who wants to die and whose family are fully agreed. The law has reasonable objections – for example, the practice could be open to very serious and criminal abuse. But where a crime is involved it is an entirely different type of case. The task for the judge, having determined the guilt, is to decide the appropriate penalty. By what criteria should s/he determine the severity of the punishment? Her various considerations will probably (depending on the character of both judge and accused) include mercy and compassion.

Such cases are exceptional and demand the most scrupulous enquiry, but are presented here as illustrating the concept that different types of evaluation may be applied at different levels and of altogether different nature. To what extent, we have to ask (not expecting an answer in our lifetime), will it be possible to resolve the moral issues of sickness, including sickness and stress generated through the Black Cloud?

And, having raised these issues, I would never venture to pontificate on the paths we may eventually need to tread. By then, however, they may be completely beyond our realm of comprehension.

But it is pointless to inveigh against the Black Cloud, since we have all taken a part, however small, in its development. The most important task is to understand it. The first point is that there is a dynamic inter-action between the Cloud and human beings. In the relatively normal situation, such as existed towards the end of the nineteenth century, a few decades after the end of the Franco-Prussian war and before the start of World War I in 1914, it was relatively weak and inoffensive.

There had, of course, been minor disturbances, but in the fairly calm atmosphere, the psychic wounds of grief could be more or less dissipated by the joys and affections of ordinary existence. But the beginning of World War I marked the start of a saturnalia of death continuing at least to the day I write. This is also a period of enormous technical development, much of it concerned with military hardware, particularly more lethal weaponry. That, of course, was part of our sad age – but just imagine a bizarre epoch in which people travelled in planes and cars, but still fought with bows and arrows!

As it is, however, whether we are actively implicated in conflict or not, we are greatly concerned with war and armaments. Many of us remember the social and political agitation seething around the now quaintly old-fashioned atom bomb! And such turmoil is in fact seldom far from our consciousnesses. Our young men are being killed in Iraq. We are expecting to be attacked by frantic Muslims in some desperate 9/11 suicide/murder outrage. And more and more people are armed to protect us.

I hope I have made the point that even if we may, thankfully, be spared the loss of a daughter or son, we share the anxiety, anger and misery of living in a world of futile and deceitful war (even if Iraq were peaceful), contributing to the opacity of the Cloud and holding back the healing that the world so badly needs.

Most people who read this, and I who write it, will dislike the Black Cloud, but even our opposition will give it some nourishment: paradoxically, we hurt ourselves, confused in our minds with love for the sufferers who contribute most to the Cloud and who bitterly oppose more muddled minds. Desperate reactions oppose their desperate source.

We are not only affected by the Cloud, but our response to it is to think and behave in a manner that creates yet more misery, as each enormity generates more of itself. And so on and so on *ad infinitum*. Thus more muddled minds and desperate reactions. Examples of such horrible cycles have become increasingly common in recent years. The most humanitarian enterprises go wrong: the US mission to help the Somalis, the war in Sierra Leone, the recent violation in the Western Congo – all are examples of the knock-on psychic principles culminating, for the time being, in mayhem in Iraq.

The great increase in violent conflict in almost the whole of Sub-Saharan Africa in the last two decades, the size of some of the armies involved, the general international tension, all these bode ill for humanity. We already have a disruption of the world's moral standards: the maltreatment of prisoners and all too often of children, the execution of hostages, mob violence and the general growth of pathological social behaviour.

The dynamic interaction between humans and the Black Cloud causes, in relatively normal times and conditions, no more stress than can be absorbed in a comparable situation today in, for example, most of Western Europe; the balance remains more or less usual. But in times of violence and uncertainty, the stress increases. That is to say, the Black Cloud also grows relatively more powerful, therefore individuals are more seriously affected. As a result they are more likely to do things that swell the Black Cloud and continue the process of escalation (as indeed is happening in many parts of the world today).

It is important to recognise the impact of people who are both outwardly strong and inwardly unsure of themselves, constantly seeking the assurance of success and riding roughshod over others who are weaker – that is to say, less self-assured, less obsessive, less ruthless, more gentle. These are the masterful tyrants in the home and, if they are astute, in administrative posts where they do great damage to their more sensitive colleagues. These people are also to be found in strategic (that is to say, powerful) positions in the police, churches, big business, crime, academia and charitable foundations (three of these categories may seem incongruous, but what matters to some of them is the power to command rather than the field in which it is exercised).

Such persons are often most intelligent, but so insensitive to others that they may act with extreme stupidity, consequently making absurd mistakes (to be blamed on subordinates who may then be dismissed for incompetence).

We are often the victims of these men in their roles of politicians and so on, but they too are victims of the Cloud. However, we are really all in the same boat with those suffering from the Cloud's miasma, and with those who take advantage of people already confused, upset or even incapacitated by it. We should cherish each other, together with the poor planet Earth. In the last few decades we have done so much, physically and psychically, to harm each other. We must bear it in mind that we are Earth's tenants, operating in a scene we are only just beginning to see clearly, but which our forebears understood in many ways so much better. And some of our present leaders, so much worse.

But we must realize that most of all these troubles are what Meister Eckhart might have called a '*Self* culture', a creature both of the Black Cloud and globalization, a planet desecrated by the conceit, greed and folly of those who have lived in it through the past century and particularly, some of those who have ruled and are now ruining it.

In concluding this section, let me turn a different ideological page and consider the culture of Islam. I am not referring to the beliefs of Al Qa'ida, which are both highly spiritual and wildly nihilistic – a strange and dubious combination. It seems as alien to the Islam of my many Muslim friends as it is to the mystical Sufism, which I greatly revere and which, I suspect, is not favoured by Al Qa'ida. But my spiritual friends begin any activity by saying with deep attention: 'In the name of God [I would say Good] the Compassionate and Merciful.'

There is no gentler balm for the malaise of the Black Cloud.

Different floors

It is always very difficult to describe states of consciousness. Those whose are what might termed 'unpleasant' – such as angry, miserable, lecherous or excited – are in general more easy to describe than those termed 'pleasant' – such as blissful, rapturous or ecstatic. Such, at least, is my experience, if that is normal. But those are the wrong adjectives, because it is not normal for me to experience them.

Let me try to describe a typical (but rare) experience.

I woke up after a rather deep afternoon rest and found myself in a different level of awareness from that in which I had gone to sleep. I saw everything quite differently. What do I mean by this? The closest I can get is that everything – the room, the furniture – had life. The things didn't move, but they shone burnished with life. I knew that I was looking into a new world.

I felt that I was at the top floor and that below me was another floor furnished with an ample supply of feelings and emotions – of awe, delight, happiness and other cheerful feelings which, ordinarily, I would have thought to indicate an exceptional, even perhaps sublime state of awareness. Now I felt they were fine, but not in any way exceptional, compared with my own consciousness.

And below this was a ground floor occupied by the sad detritus of the Black Cloud, aware only of misery, jealousy, confusion, anger, a horrid stew of negative feelings.

Approach to therapy meditation

The programme set out below can probably act as a pattern for users needing further confidence or insight before taking another step in what might be a difficult or risky enterprise in such fields as politics, the economy, or social development.

I would propose:

1 Begin with something neutral, harmless and desirable such as treatment for a 'bad back' or some other not serious condition.
2 Then look at the strains, tension, bad posture, etc. Observe with attentive detachment, which is actually a form of meditation. Do this until you feel comfortable with it, not fussed.
3 The meditation is woven through gradual stages around the decluttering of the mind, first, simply observing the mind as it is, strictly *not* making any judgement of good or bad. Forget the back pain (or whatever was the original minor trouble). It has served its purpose, and will diminish or depart.
4 Concentrate on the Mind of the Universe as incorporating Everything. Don't try to map it mentally. Just observe it. Or let it observe you. Envelop the Black Cloud in the Mind and watch it diminish and, if you do the exercise regularly, disappear.
6 Notice the diminution, and hopefully complete disappearance, of the original pain.
7 Maintain the practice and take up a role in whatever field you feel you can best serve.

I want to emphasise that I would blame the group or nation, such as I have been referring to, for fundamental responsibility for its cruel practices. They may be the unavoidable consequences of past happenings. Nazi Germany, for example, virtually vanished after the Nuremburg trials, and was not resurrected, thus demonstrating its cure from the Nazi vice. Had it persisted, however, it would demonstrate a more deep-seated psychological infection.

Growth

There is nothing to compare with the mysterious recognition of change and growth in oneself. It may come in childhood and youth, not so much in maturity (we tend to be absorbed in adult responsibilities) and then again in greater age. One episode came at an amazingly peaceful period after a terrible war which all expected to conclude with vengeful massacres. Several others which I won't specify have come during this writing, pondering on the enigmas of doors being opened I had thought locked.

To begin the brief journey of our lives, many of us will bring happily to mind the circumstances of birth and childhood, It begins, of course, with the universal and wonderful miracle: the egg and sperm of our parents coming together to form a living Being. At first, and for a number of years, we are a sack of skin within which develop a vast number of different potentials for thoughts, love, actions, skills, memories, and so on.

Out of all this emerges a baby, who fairly soon becomes someone, a 'character', whom we all appreciate as a real person called Mary or John. The parents are delighted but don't like comments about the word 'person' coming from the Latin for mask, and hence an actor who conceals a genuine boy or girl. S/he is just their beloved baby.

And as the years pass, the 'personality' of M or J becomes increasingly clear until we notice the diversity that we have already discussed: the diversity of our child – the artistic sensibility, the surprising toughness, the quality of mercy which is not strained. And more yet of course, a wonderful abundance of potential and actual talents. I would particularly like to stress the mercy. This lays emphasis on spiritual qualities which transcend the logic of law with humane judgment.

The very great spirits, mainly of the past, seem to have come up the hard way. The two I mentioned certainly did. Nelson Mandela did twenty-seven years in a South African gaol. The Mahatma had years of battling with a racist legal system. And how many unknown others were there?

I like to think, perhaps scientifically, that the Mind of the Universe, which I greatly believe in, locates the essence which is thrusting upwards through the Black Clouds (which in some way are universal too). And they touch and attract each other. But do they, the Mandelas, know anything above this? I suspect not. So did Meister Eckhart, but not very scientifically – which I sense, was right.

Human relations

All the issues I want to consider are basically those of human relationships. The relationships between parents, especially mothers, and children and those between women and men are the foundation on which all things, including the great and terrible ones, like war, are established. So I make bold to talk of the relations of the genders. I am not of course a woman, so have to base what I say on what I have learned from and been taught by women. I owe so much to them and apologise to them for what I have misunderstood.

(I assume a relationship of respect, affection and attraction between the woman and the man. Sadly there are too many relationships marred by contempt, fear and domination.)

The contact begins, let's assume, with a measure at least of liking. One or other kisses or affectionately touches the other. They talk in a friendly fashion – and here we must allow an interval of time which in my limited experience and dependant on circumstances may last between minutes and any length of time.

The next stage, however long it has taken to attain, is one in which probably each feels enough trust and liking for the other to give or accept words or actions which will show it. The words and the fondling make it clear that a strong relationship is starting to develop.

This is also a period in which specifically sexual factors become dominant. Fully aroused sexuality is very powerful. Speaking only as a man (but assuming that women are not greatly different) this is a stage of very sensitive arousal; the penis, being outside the body, is in a state of constant provocation. It suffers also, but entrancingly, during the sexual act. It is swollen and responsive and longs to discharge its semen in a culminating spasm, yet paradoxically grieves when this has happened.

This is a point at which, perhaps for fear of jeopardising a marriage, one or other party may withdraw, or make it clear that, while remaining good friends, s/he must not let the relationship go further.

Assuming, however, that there are no impediments, the nature of the relationship will change. Some partners may feel that a probationary period has come to an end. Up until now each has a slight sense of being on trial, sexually and generally. Now they feel confirmed (though sadly some never so) they can allow themselves to speak and act as they feel inclined both sexually and in general. This is often a stage of extravaganza when all sorts of psycho-sexual peculiarities are revealed, and it is hoped accepted with love and understanding

It is also a period of great fulfilment. A strong building block for society has been created.

Love

It is an extraordinary thing that in no country in the world is there any formal recognition of the supreme place of Love. Nowhere, certainly, is there anything like a Ministry of Love, not even a tiny little cupboard where some very junior official comes for even an hour every three weeks to – to what? To open the letters (there are none) and to dust the empty files... I am really surprised, shaken and ashamed that we don't officially recognise love as something to treat seriously and officially (perhaps not officially) but as earnestly as health or education. But not to acknowledge publicly *love* – to which we owe our being, which we hope to enjoy in full measure, and which we would all strive to protect and promote above everything else – shows a monstrous neglect for each of us individually and collectively. Any cabinet which does not have a very senior minister for love (no, not for love *affairs*) should resign en bloc. All right, laugh scornfully and then get on with something important like – well, like war which is only significant because it leads to thousands of men and women losing the people they love. But let's move away from this approach to love, to one less likely to promote flippant wisecracks.

I mean by this the Universe, the very exemplar of love on a gigantic scale, constant yet adaptable, circling suns as a planet and as sun-mother providing stability to the child planets. And as our own sun providing so much that we need of heat and shade, of light and warmth, and of frost and cold in due season. What we do know is that we don't know what the distant future may hold for us. What we do know is that many happenings of the last few decades demonstrate that there has been a very serious deficit of love, or distorted expression of love, which appears likely to deteriorate through, for example, excessively greedy use of fossil fuels

Coming right back to us humans, there is no need to argue that love is of crucial importance in our lives, from the moment we are born to our loving mother until we die happy in the love of family or friends. But in between, things can go wrong. I don't pretend to act the psychiatrist. I know, however, that when human relations go wrong the blame lies with the two minds of the couple or more people concerned.

Love, by contrast, is clear and powerful. This is a very frequent theme, I believe, of all the major religions. It is expressly and beautifully expressed by Paul of Tarsus. But an individual whose mind is in part affected, whether at birth or as a result of subsequent traumatic experience, cannot live harmoniously with others or with a single other. They may manage for a while, but their relations will be to some extent be marred by mutual incomprehension.

But there are certainly cases when a man or woman of clear mind and exceptionally good heart will wish to live with and bring comfort and solace to someone quite incompatible. Such persons are, to use an antique phrase, the salt of the earth.

To complete these paragraphs on love, I return briefly to the fanciful discussion of a minister of love. This woman or man would need to be a good lover in the sense of being both sensually ardent, and affectionately loving. (The identification of these qualities might require both tact and ingenuity.) The practitioners with whom s/he will work could be of many professional persuasions and his/her job would be to ensure that they had the support and opportunities for professional enhancement which would contribute to the development of the many-layered profession.

It is obvious that the professional work of this minister would not differ substantially from that of most others. There is, however, an additional range of responsibility: that of liaison with the relevant departments of foreign countries and their missions in Britain. The reason for this is that the world is in a fluid and combustible state, the fantasies of confused minds need to be understood, both by the country or countries concerned, and by the great international agencies, but also by our own government. This minister, then, would play a key part in global affairs. All the more important, therefore, that the insights of widely agreed 'religious' principles should be recognised and applied.

Let's not deceive ourselves, however.

Most aspects of *hatred* can be simply disposed of as the opposite or absence of love: 'He's a snob so of course I hate him'. Or 'I don't care in the least about X; he can slit his throat or not as far as I'm concerned'.

The first may be thought of as institutional hatred, dislike for another only because of her/his attributes (language, appearance, etc.). This may be dissolved by dissociating the classification from the personal attributes through association, and may lead to liking.

The second is harder to build on, because there is no emotional potential. By contrast, the collective psychological coercive force of a whole Nazi regiment could create an almost impregnable moral identification.

Hostilities and love

Changing signs of the times

The signs of the times have made me increasingly pessimistic about finding firm grounds for encouragement over the state of the world. It is no longer possible to be sure that we can survive another two or three decades without a nuclear war, or much beyond this century without vast environmental disasters, including flooding, a poisonous atmosphere, contaminated food and water, and a civilization degenerating into many lethal struggles between desperate armed groups raiding or being raided by each other (which has already been happening). Some of these may be expected to maintain or establish sovereignty over smaller and more precarious territories already whittled away by environmental disasters. We have, of course, had alarming previews of much of this during the last few decades.

I have reluctantly reached these unhappy conclusions for the reasons set out in the numbered paragraphs below, as well as from personal experience of some of the factors mentioned.

I cannot, however, emphasise sufficiently that the obverse of the arguments for disaster are the reasons for peace. They are within us, peace is within us, the more we share peace the more will peace have the strength eventually to prevail as the normal condition of our lives. And this is a prerequisite for the ultimate inner peace. Meanwhile, however, there are compelling reasons for pessimism. For example:

1   For the last few hundred years some of the mainly Christian and European nations have been dominated by mercantile ambitions. Among other practices, the slave trade (in which some engaged) was a key activity damaging the slaves, those who traded in them and the areas from which they were torn. This is not mentioned solely for its genuine social or moral reprehensibility, but for the disruptive effects on the societies concerned.
2   The greed that stimulated the slave trade, and of course many other forms of commerce, had the effect of dehumanising those involved in the trade. Their minds were cluttered and confused by materialistic obsessions.
3   Commerce, particularly large-scale and international commerce, became increasingly impersonal. The 'family business' changed into a great corporation engaged in gigantic operations concealed from the normal eye.
4   This development, coupled with vastly improved communications,

contributed signally to well-named globalization. The activities of the wealthy nations and/or corporations expanded everywhere that profit was to be made. The infection of greed that stifles humane considerations spread to many minds of those having few chances of wealth, thus creating stimulus for bitterness and resentment.

5 To sum up developments so far: the objectives of this evolving mercantile civilization could be described as 'Profit and Power'. These have become the mantras of the present age.

6 Hundreds of millions have been excluded by poverty and/or custom from the echoing mantra. But whereas in the past (even the recent past as I have known it), they were more or less satisfied with their life, though some of them complained that the 'establishment' accused them of 'holding back progress'. And indeed some of them did feel left out. Often they were resentful and angry, lacking the mantra symbols, perhaps especially the power. That sense of loss is not, of course, uncommon. But at this stage, the investments, bargains, goods and other trinkets created by the wealthy vendors must be constantly evolved or elaborated to keep in the market. Take the trivial example of the mobile phone which is developing so rapidly and advertised so craftily that when some fresh gimmick is invented, a young person feels 'out of it' if s/he doesn't have the new model also. All this adds to the confusion and ambivalence of what had once been unruffled minds. And also drives the engine of capitalism faster and more recklessly.

7 On the international scale, the USA as a whole wants oil in the same way that the youngster wants a new mobile phone, and will go to extreme lengths to obtain it – and then what? Colonise Mars? And *then* what? Take control of some other country's wells, of course. (And of course that is happening already.)

8 I envisage an enormous balloon that is blown up and up and up until it bursts; a point we have almost reached. But the bursting point doesn't mean that everything will settle down. We will instead go through a period of chaotic confusion, uncertainty, anger and no doubt carnage.

9 What we need is someone of the calibre of Nelson Mandela, who truly knows what is happening and so is able to take real action. In his absence, however, let me say something which the partisans of both (or however many) parties might consider.

10 We have got it all wrong (except several million women and men of all genuine faiths and many different societies). We have all wanted things (different according to taste); our illusion is believing that happiness can be gained by doing, seeing, hearing, smelling, etc. – but primarily, of course, *having*. I learnt as a small child that *having* only lasted a short while, until replaced by another 'want'. In fact, however, it depends on *being*, being aware of the real life and spirit within us and our fellow humans, not of the world of the ads.

(Let me emphasise, however, that this is not to decry the wonderful emotions of love and appreciation; or grief at death or illness. On the contrary, the expression and the awareness of these feelings within us can do much to help, encourage, or comfort others – but this cannot happen if we are absorbed in worrying, or wanting, or dislikes, or selfish dreaming.)

11 There are many things in the mind which are not conducive to happiness or satisfaction (this obviously is why we are unhappy). The thing not to do, however, is *not* to buy a treat to cheer yourself up, but to get rid of the emotion (fear, dislike, misery) that was understandably upsetting you.

12 When you have clarified your mind on the issues we have been discussing here, you will have gone a long way towards some clarification of the tangled emotions which had been so distressing. You may wish to talk to a teacher of meditation, or indeed anyone who shares your concerns.

13 This is now a lucky number! The teacher may be of any faith (or apparently, none); even a Quaker.

The hurricane

The world was severely shocked and shaken by two events in the autumn of 2004.

One was extremely obvious and destructive, causing a great deal of damage, but relatively little loss of life, over a large area of the Caribbean and the southern states of the USA.

The other was in a remote and obscure area of Caucasian Russia where a ruthless gang of crazed fanatics killed 500 people, mostly children (and including themselves). This too drew the horrified attention of most of the rest of the world.

In most ways these two incidents appear to be entirely divorced, but I believe there is a connecting factor which is, in fact, the reason for writing this book.

The reason for the hurricane is by far the easier. It is climatic. (Though that, of course is very complex, with sinister forebodings for the future of the planet.) But in this case the 'natural' conditions are intensified by a human factor: excessive and increasing use of fossil fuels. And there is at least a two-pronged cause for this: American addiction to the motor car together with President Bush's rejection of the Kyoto Treaty for political and/or 'scientific' reasons. And perhaps at least partly because of the powerful oil interests of influential members of his administration.

There is nothing possibly comparable that I can suggest for the crazy, wicked, heroic – choose your epithet – assassins of the school except possibly emphasizing sympathy for the Chechens and other local peoples.

There is, however, a much more general psychological factor. Most Protestants and, by nationalistic contagion, a fair proportion of Catholics share that aspect of the protestant ethic identified by the title of R.H. Tawney's enlightening *Religion and the Rise of Capitalism*. Here there is a sharp disagreement with Islam: a good Muslim should – and many do – pay a fixed proportion of his income as Zakat, the recognized and considerable religious tax.

Turning to the 'terrorists', they presumably came from a Muslim background, and if so, as has usually been the case, unorthodox: murder is inexcusable. But the English should regret with great shame the slaughter of supposed witches by 'good' Christians in seventeenth-century New England. We must, therefore, be cautious judges.

It is perhaps more difficult to understand the motives of the Caucasus killers, as they might be termed for lack of identification. They do seem, however, possibly to have had different origins. Were they selected haphazardly, or through some careful process of choice? Probably the latter, which implies the existence of an organization such as that which planned and selected the 9/11 pilots for training and performance. In this last case I am surprised and moved to think of the young wife, who must have sustained a horrifying shock on discovering her husband's role in the terrible affair.

But what were the motives of the actor or actors? I have recently read what is supposedly a children's book – *The Amber Spyglass*, by Philip Pullman. (Which I would also recommend as a wonderful creation.) The author's potential assassin is trained by a high ecclesiastical *superior* to murder a young girl, supposed to be guilty of dreadful evil. He is given a sort of pre-emptive absolution for killing her in a hypothetical future. (I am glad to say he does not succeed.) In real life, two 'terrorists' who asked for some concession for the children were immediately shot by the leader of the group. This may be a further proof (borne out by other survivors) of the heterogeneous nature of the group.

It may not be easy to round up these young people. Still less so to get to know them and to detain them until they have talked freely, and opened their hearts and understanding.

I would predict of both sides that if captured and interrogated, and if they have important information, they will either deny their knowledge, or weave a confusing tissue of lies. The best way to get information is to make friends – and discover that you are fond of your enemy. Your superior officers may not approve of this method, but then they probably won't get the information they want, or a deceptive version of it.

Now there is the question of motive. The present Allies hope to defeat their enemies and then, so far as is possible given bitterness and anger, to rebuild the fractured relationship. It is most encouraging to remember the generous and constructive magnanimity of the Allies after World War II, mainly the USA, to Germany and Japan. The present rather nebulous allies, apart from Britain and the US (and formerly Spain), have no tangible enemies, perhaps apart from North Korea, Iran and – just possibly and most embarrassingly – in a couple of years, Iraq.

I believe, however, that Britain, the US and various other countries with Muslim institutions should immediately launch a great effort (as may have been done already) to repair the most serious rupture of faith and friendship between

Muslim and non-Muslim groups including, of course, Al Qa'ida, and militant groups in Palestine and elsewhere. This would be difficult and dangerous, politically and physically. But I am certain it must be attempted, otherwise the whole world will within a few decades go up in flames, damaged beyond repair – en route for becoming a Black Hole!

This chapter has hitherto not touched on the main issues we have been considering – emptiness and the Black Cloud. The collective mind of the 'terrorists' is swamped by the passions of hatred, violence and perhaps fear; their mental opacity has obliterated all openness to other human beings.

The local people, mostly the parents of the unhappy children, are demented by grief and anxiety. It would be almost impossible for them to disentangle their minds from the ghastly material present.

Certainly the others, mostly overshadowed by the awesome present and the probably imminent death of many of the injured, could hardly cling to any surviving elements of detachment and compassion.

How, moreover, could any of them, any of either party, fend off the insidious advances of the Black Cloud? – and this is the core of the discussion. The muddled confusion, the ideals – absurd or deluded – that invaded their intelligence, took them, metaphorically and many of them literally, 'out of this world'.

War

These pages bravely (or foolhardily) suggest that there is an alternative to war as a means of settling disputes. This is not only wise diplomacy, although that certainly can help, or simply more war, which almost always doesn't. It suggests, contrary to the view of many professors of international relations and some politicians, a very different approach. First, however, we have to deal with a serious and fundamental problem. A problem of two Minds. The first is the Mind of the Universe, the ever-lasting Mind, the source of all wisdom and knowledge. The other is the mind of humanity, a fragment of Mind, partly detached and corrupted by the rapacity and anguish of a tormented world, which now hovers, suffering yet hopeful, over the planet, receiving messages of increasing horror, and incapable of returning much comfort. Its restoration is part of our responsibility.

At the moment we are skirting round the fringe of war and the miserable horrors that it brings, the destructively confused emotions, and the helpless despair it generates; also, of course, the compensatory courage, nobility and sacrifice it evokes – but not, alas, enough to make up for the deadening loss. War is alive and well.

It is the dread of every human being, save for those unhappy souls whose minds are addled with hectic fantasies of violence. And yet we are all implicated. The mind of humanity is one in its confusion, pain and bewilderment. But it is a mind mainly created by ourselves. Even the millions who long and work for peace share to some extent the heavy mass of a collective mind scared, unhappy and addled with the incompatible. If I may use myself as an example, I worked hard lifelong for peace in a dozen grim theatres – and served for five years as a soldier in World War II! Such apparent contradiction between peace work and soldiery may well be fairly common. In the periods of, and between, the two world wars, millions of men and their families worldwide shared comparable attitudes; these included acceptance of war as the price to pay for peace. They shared this ambivalence in very different proportions according to age, education, family, etc.: the fear, misery, boredom, hopelessness, hope, love, irritation, yearning and dislikes (hatred was fairly uncommon). They all experienced it.

This collective mind was not particularly emphatic (except for men safe in their bunkers) in the sense that the Nazi mind in its heyday was violent. Otherwise the mind was muddled and uncertain, aware of the limitations and crude naivety of old-fashioned militarism, but drawn by its frank simplicity – 'Come on lads, let's just go in and polish the whole lot off. No more argy bargy. Then we'll have a cup of tea.' And it's now even more confused. Even very clever men think we can protect ourselves with weapons which, if used, could wipe us all out. What an absurd contradiction!

In previous and indeed subsequent pages, I have made more mention of the Black Cloud than of the infinite, the boundless Mind of the Universe. My only excuse is that the former impinges upon us so noticeably through the force of its local impact. However, when we do recognize it, we must wonder at its beneficence. I cannot, however, believe that this wonderful spirit could flow guilty of favouritism. Our sibling stars and planets must have countless differing needs, though doubtless of a very varied type.

But the American Civil War soldier, General Sherman, said, 'War is Hell'. He was, so to speak, dead right. Much later there was the inexorable horror of the Somme (my mother heard the guns from the hospital bed in Seine et Oise where I was born). And of course there is an endless list of the victims of tyranny: the millions slain in concentration camps; the Gypsies of Eastern Europe; all who heard the gloating threat, 'We know how to make you talk'; the 800,000 slaughtered by the Interahamwe; the endless victims of Pol Pot; the Caucasus killings; Saddam Hussein; Stalin; Mobutu; and the victims of the many little known but equally execrable tyrants (and I would include, though not in the same class, Tony Blair, who to satisfy George Bush's whim, joined him in a war both foolish and shameless). And many, many other people and places such as Guatemala (happily now restored), Vietnam and Salvador. But there is no end to the list of places where lives were miserably lost.

But they are actually not lost. They live in the memories they leave behind. Many of them are still bodily alive, but some damaged in mind, as were so many survivors of the Korean and other wars. And there are the dead, both those who survived and those who did not.

All these, I am certain, constitute a collective mind, a wounded, angry mind adding to the Black Cloud hovering above us to blot out the light of reality; a mind that sends and receives messages – of pain to the living coupled with further confusion, and upwards to the cloud, reinforcing angry befuddlement. I am convinced that the disturbed abnormalities of our global society merely project its anguish: the myriad wars like pustules of blood, the angry lust for profit and power, the enslavement of the weak and wretched, the insidious spread of appetite and craving even among small children. These are surely the signs of a sick society.

(Why has this situation not arisen before? Surely other ages have known others comparably awful? The simple answer is that the numbers have been much smaller. The weight of misery, for example, has never been nearly so heavy. Nothing was more ghastly than the massacres decreed by Genghiz Khan, but the number of victims was minute by comparison with the great killing sprees of the twentieth century.)

I am suggesting, in fact, that the voice of the dead, whether a psychic phenomenon transmitted from the Cloud, or nurtured in the mind of a loved one, is the true voice of war. Why not peace? Because war, horrible war, has embedded itself in our minds. Peace is difficult, it's an ideal to be indulged in one day when we have conquered our enemies. So we must get on with the job and build all the weapons that cruel silly Saddam never really had (except to gas Kurds).

The upshot is that we can't have peace until we have eradicated war. But is this really true? If we really believe that disarmament is primarily a psychological rather than a political problem, although a hellishly difficult one, let's get on with it. But let us never forget the Black Cloud, the damage our kind has inflicted on the true Mind, and our duty to restore it.

Let me now, to fulfil part of the promise made at the start of this chapter, try to suggest a strategy for weakening the moral and intellectual hold that war has rudely seized over human communities. This ugly scourge has come to present itself as noble and heroic.

The first step is to strip away its pretensions and to display it as unambiguously destructive – though not the people who wage it. But there is an even more powerful argument. As you explore further you will begin to understand that it is psychologically inaccurate to describe someone in terms of what you may assess by some adjective, pleasant or not. This, you will judge, is no more than a figment of the fluid mind. To identify a human being, essentially an emanation of the Great Mind, in terms of one or two possibly very trivial of her/his attributes, is ridiculous. To grasp this will be a step towards eradicating the sources of violence and anger in our hearts and minds. This, you will soon discover, is simply a verbal habit picked on casually, which becomes a derogatory nickname (poor old So-and-So, a bit of an ass). This you will discover becomes a part of the family or community patois.

A dispassionate examination will show that these practices are at least partly irrational: the actual process of enquiry will be likely to weaken them and provide the mental spade with which deeper to dig their roots out.

Continue the 'research' further, but preferably with another group of people who by training are professionally practised in violence, such as soldiers and policemen. I have come to know several very senior officers (some of whom were also in fact heads of state) who were devoted to both the skills and the ideals of Conflict Transformation. Such persons are usually, but not always, workers with whom we would do well to share skills, and collaborate.

The philosopher's views – and fate

Our planet earth is a part of the solar system, while the solar system is part of an unimaginably vast universe in which we are now able to observe events of millions of years ago. Nevertheless, we are connected with this gigantic system in which innumerable cosmic rays (whose purpose and origin are largely unknown) create a web of connectedness. There are other forms of energy which our astronomical instruments can record but interpret little, except those within our solar system. Some of these distinguish it and have a known effect, such as the seasons, while on a smaller scale the moon's influence is very obvious – the tides, for example, and the migration of birds and other creatures.

Undoubtedly the interaction between earth and moon is rich and complex, and to some extent unknown – except for myths of madness! But it would be surprising if age-old tales of lunacy were mere myth and if this were not just the surface of a deep, but not necessarily crazy, impact.

I have very tentatively considered the possibility of some sort of psychic lunar link between the minds before and/or after death. But this is just an interesting possibility, or even perhaps probability. What I hold as a certainty, however, is that the happenings on the earth for the last ten thousand years, since agricultural settlements were established, must have had a dominating effect on the collective human mind. I am speaking of intelligence in the sense of the ability to deal sensibly with the available resources, whatever they were; which, depending on the date and the stage of scientific development, may be to make, say, a spear or a computer.

But we have used our skills in other sorts of ways. The impetus that drove us to improve the plough was less to grow more crops than to sell more of them and live in greater luxury. In particular we wanted to have more fields and sell more food to our neighbours and then to protect ourselves from them because they were jealous, and might try to take our house or village, so we had better stop them first.

And so it goes on until now.

For the last two or three thousand years the movement has been relatively regular. There have been periods of great blood letting, the terrible campaigns of the Mongol invasions, for example. But even the Napoleonic wars were not particularly disruptive to Europe. It wasn't until 1914 that the most sanguinary century took its toll. The worst, however, was not until 1945 when the Second World War ended; then its particularly murderous epoch began. It was only in the sixty or so years since then that the full horror of the world's condition became clear – at least to those with eyes to see the carnage and ears to hear the groans of global grief.

But to those even without the baubles of affluence, it was a period of jet travel, of smart cars, absurd wealth for the already wealthy (and footballers), alcohol and drugs. The poor were better off financially than in some places, but because the rich were relatively so much richer than ever, they felt and indeed were much poorer.

Now the rich *and* the poor, and in fact most people of all sorts and conditions (except a sense of reality), were making a lethal mistake. They both believed, though with varying conviction, that Happiness could be bought – by hard work, by obeying the rule (every sort of rule), by pleasing someone (like God), by having 'what I want most in the world'.

This is the universal insanity, the basic misconception of everything, of reality. It's very democratic. Rich and poor, brilliantly clever and abysmally stupid are at last (or always have been) together.

I should stress that I am not just parroting scores of serious articles about the state of the world. Although I lacked the amount of statistical evidence, I felt that what I had personally seen and heard was enough to make valid judgements on events. Much that I experienced was evocative and enlightening beyond the ability of facts and figures to tell the whole truth. These alone cannot either illuminate or elucidate the depth and passions of human behaviour.

Excitement and, for many, wealth were the goals. So were new machines and new ideas of what was desirable; and just forgetting what was good, in favour of what was attractive. Too much of what was attractive was also bad, and the powerful became frightened of the poor and underprivileged – who then also gave them good reason to be afraid. And because the poor were both unwise and desperate, they built new religions which said that killing, which had been proclaimed as bad, was good.

'And that's why my friend here is going to shoot me with his pistol. This is bad for me but also for him because his brain is just as clotted as my ancestor's when he thought the new plough would bring everlasting happiness. But it only brought him confusion – the same confusion and element of good sentimental clotting that will come over my friend when he has shot me. Actually, however, it's already there, otherwise he would not see any point in shooting me.'

These were the last words of a Teacher, who had gone around trying to help people suffering the newly defined sickness of Cluttered Mind. And this is what he taught: most people had lost touch with reality. They no longer valued the truth, hated those who did and became crazy. They hated the teachers and soon there were very few. The crazed people were frightened, forgetting the wisdom they had always been taught. And being frightened and foolish, they did the foolish and desperate things which built up fear and hatred, selfishness and confusion, which meant that their destruction, both inflicted and suffered, became somewhere between probable and inevitable.

But it's more complicated than that, because in the muddled mess of the conflicted Mind, there remained an element of the wisdom that is inherent in the human being. This must be protected and cared for like a precious plant, being also ours.

Black Cloud – captivity

Towards the end of World War II it was clear that over a hundred thousand men had been captured in early 1940, mostly in Dunkirk (those taken later by the Japanese were not included in the arrangements to be described here). Senior military officers who had been prisoners of war (POWs) in World War I appealed to the authorities saying that their experiences had ruined their lives, and that something must be done to help prisoners in World War II to avoid what they had gone through.

The government agreed to set up what were called Civil Resettlement Units (CRUs) of which 120 were established. This I think was the first organization officially set up to counteract a particular aspect of the mental misery we call the Black Cloud. The reasons why the captured soldiers suffered particular traumas were analysed particularly subtly by a psychologist; most of the others were psychiatrists, while I was the research officer.

We examined a wide perspective of social issues and came up with what seemed pretty well correct then, and still does today over sixty years later. The essence of it was that the men had been uprooted from their social soil a number of times, some of them very painful. The word we used for this was 'desocialisation', a hideous but in the circumstances practical word, meaning that the individual no longer feels that he belongs to the group which he is officially 'a part of'.

To start with, a new soldier was 'dug up' from his family. This was usually in any case painful, but also to some extent potentially upsetting; it entailed a shift in the pattern of kinship relationships based on affection and habit, to one based on impersonal and authoritarian structure.

Further down the scale of size, our young (but not always) soldier becomes a member of the very tight-knit society of a few men who know that their lives may depend on the skill and loyalty of their immediate partners.

But now his mates are dead or captured and sent elsewhere. His roots are not only dug up but destroyed. He is back in an anonymous and amorphous group, in which he finds it much harder to 'belong'.

But eventually comes peace, a return home and, if they choose to volunteer, the CRUs. Anyone who had been a prisoner of war in Europe would be welcome to join it. The men were given every sort of medical and practical help over homes, jobs or purchases (the world was very different from the one they had left).

They were given a free pass to travel home at weekends. It seemed important that these visits should be fairly brief so that acclimatization would be gradual (experience showed that going straight home could disastrously overload the emotions). They also had job rehearsals which gave them a taste of what it was like to be a teacher, train driver, farmer, grocer, policeman, jockey and so on.

But the basic question, after a few weeks, was: Is he doing well both at home and at work?

This was my department. The question we asked was crucial. We began with the idea that the CRU experience was supposed to enable men whose recent life had been at least to some extent destabilizing, to cope with the emotional and/or social demands on their mental balance. After weeks (or months – I'm no longer quite sure) of long meetings with their families, friends, neighbours, partners, it seemed sensible to assess, as well as the men themselves, their relations with anyone with whom they had contact. How else could we know how they were getting on?

We started by meeting and talking only with people who had *not* had the CRU experience, the supposed norm for our sample. These were straightforward, responsible men (and a very few women).

It was, however, surprising and encouraging that the 'best' product of the CRUs were the most progressively constructive and tolerant of any of the people we met, including responsible men who had not been in the army at all! The relationships of this CRU sample with family and friends, with colleagues and bosses were friendly and positive. By contrast, some of the rest found it very hard to develop constructive and friendly relations. They responded very little compared with most of the others and there were a few painful cases of violent rages and rather frantic crimes. On the whole, however, we felt the experiment had been quietly successful.

It is naturally to be hoped that the need for such institutions as the CRUs will not recur. If they do, however, and not necessarily in the military context, we may hope that our experience shows, in however small a way, how to resist the forces of the Black Cloud and to steer society back on its proper course.

Casus belli

The following trivial incident, accurately recorded here, illustrates on a minute scale the petty beginning of what can become a bloody war.

Not many years ago A, irritated because of some frustrating banking regulation, walked out of the bank leaving his walking stick behind. Shortly the bank manager phoned to say he was keeping the stick until A came to collect it.

It so happened that A was delayed for several days and the manager phoned him again to say that they still had the stick and that another client of the bank, Mr B, hasd seen the stick and thought it was his, and supposed that A had taken B's stick in error. The manager phoned A again, suggesting a meeting at the bank to exchange the sticks. This was agreed by A, and a date was fixed. It should be noted that A is hard of hearing and that he did not grasp what he was being told about B's stick. He really only apprehended the date and the recovery of his stick.

No one seems to have wondered at this or indeed a later stage, how it was that A could have taken B's stick before B came to the bank with his own stick and noticed that of A.

A arrived at the RV (to use the military convention) punctually at 11 am.

B was already there. The actual verbal sequence has not been recorded, but in the melée of words, both of allegation and defence, the key note was accusation by B (possibly supported by the manager) of A for not bringing his stick for the exchange. (In fact, assuming that if he did so and recovered the other stick as he expected, he would be encumbered by them both when he went later, as intended, to do some shopping. This, however, was not mentioned.) As it was, however, there was perhaps a general assumption that he had cheated on the agreement, tacit on the part of the bank, vocal from B.

A tried to explain that he had not brought the stick to be returned to its rightful owner, B, because it was not, and had never been, in the bank. Anyway it was an utterly different type of stick which could never be mistaken for either A's or B's.

B tried to explain that the stick that he had brought to be returned to A could never have been his, because it was too long: it must really have been A's because he was taller.

At this stage the talk was becoming wilder and more incoherent. No one was listening to anyone else.

The manager, however, broke in firmly, saying, 'This is a place for banking, not this sort of argument.'

Everyone agreed, and A just walked out, giving up all claims to his walking stick, although convinced it was his own. Each probably felt wronged by the other.

It might have been helpful for A to say to B, 'Lets get out of this place and have a drink somewhere so we can sort all this out sensibly.' But he didn't.

In this simple, foolish story there are several lessons to be learnt.

The first is to act quickly and thoughtfully, not to wait around and just let things happen.

The second is to understand the other side's point of view.

Next, to share and consult with a third party (in this case the manager).

Fourth, to assume the other party has a case; try to understand it, using as much intelligent sympathy as you can muster. Consult with her/him personally if possible, and if not through a neutral intermediary.

Observe and control your own hostile and self-righteous feelings.

Finally, remember Churchill's dictum: Jaw, Jaw, not War, War.

Remember also that the Black Cloud is addicted to violence. Try to avoid being drawn in.

Conflict Transformation

The preceding sections of this short work provide the basis of the ideals, ideas and practice of Conflict Transformation (CT) which is now generally thought to be a more accurate representation of what used to be called Conflict Resolution or Peace Making.

It used to be a matter of bargaining or bullying the opposite number (ON), but we now feel that this entirely contravenes what should be the spirit. After all, ON and his/her associates are fellow human beings, we are part of each other. It is in our common interest to come to conclusions that are just and constructive. If ON has had the misfortune to be mistakenly informed, it is our responsibility to show him/her a happier way. It is our privilege to help our would-be colleague in this respect.

We will, of course, explore together the minutiae of the settlement we are working towards. There will certainly be details affecting the social conditions, the political structure, the economic objectives of ON. We may not agree on all of them, and perhaps this may be because we have been wrongly or insufficiently informed. This can of course be corrected. But what if ON is intransigent on matters which we feel crucial? Suppose, for example, ON's colleagues have aspirations which involve war or enslaving other groups? If we cannot affect his implacable designs, we shall have to break off the negotiations – but not the relationship. We will continue to press for a change. We note that dramatic shifts in policy do sometimes occur, sometimes for the worse, unfortunately, but by no means always.

In our contacts with ON the happiness of the people is a constant theme. In fact we are always interested and eager to discuss the nature of happiness with ON. If, for example, the people of a particular nation are very keen on alcohol, is it the duty of the authorities to make it as cheap and easily available as possible – thus also gaining in popularity? Presumably we would feel it our duty to reason against such a move, at the risk of losing popularity. An even more crucial issue would be belligerence. What stance should we adopt if our ON's nation appears implacably bent on war? Do we cast it off, as we might a seriously errant son? Certainly not, even if we incur opprobrium, indeed even if the aggressor actually assaults us.

In such a lamentable pass, we can only hope that our nerve does not fail, that our friends continue to understand us, that the conflict is eventually transformed and that peace prevails.

There may, however, be a different way out of this impasse. Instead of either seeking more common interests, or agreeing dubiously to differ, play a completely separate game. We state firmly that we are not interested in the subterfuges and compromises which we have been fiddling with and bickering over. We could no doubt eventually cobble together some passionless compromise which no one is particularly keen on or interested in, and which therefore falls apart before very long.

No. We set our sights on ambitious and exciting targets that people have dreamed about for years, but always in the end discarded because they lacked the courage and imagination to begin this particular enterprise. Now, however, we are determined to go ahead.

If the other party were to join as an equal partner, certainly not as the leader but also not as a subordinate, they would be welcomed and we would begin planning immediately once the crucial agreement has been reached.

Well, OK, but just what does that really mean?

It means that there are no soft options for directors and such like.

What else is so important about it?

Its objective.

And what is that?

Happiness.

Most people gasp, many of them sceptically. But the spokespersons are not worried. They claim that several measures would contribute to the harmony and happiness of the enterprise, apart from normal provisions for very good working conditions. But having happiness as the objective of the work and its products would introduce a sense of purpose and even, they hope, idealism. They believe that these factors will contribute considerably to effective work and job satisfaction.

At this moment someone asks a diffident question.

We have listened with great interest, but I don't think we have been told the nature and purpose of this enterprise. Perhaps you could enlighten us?

The spokespersons laugh merrily. 'Good question,' they say. 'We don't know. We began to speculate about these issues when we were working on a particular commercial conflict. And we were very dissatisfied with the lack of progress. We then did some further exploration in industry, schools, and international conflicts. Some of our experiences have been very promising, as a result of which we are continuing enthusiastically.

'Now perhaps we could consider working together to identify situations on which you feel our approach would be most effective.'

Evil?

Are some people evil? Is evil a sort of ultimate *Ungood* reserved for those we believe to be much more than straightforwardly wicked, but monstrosities seeming, though not actually *being*, human.

But the concept outlined in the first part of these explorations leads a different way. As individuals we are like a group of actors; one is the hero, then the heroine, the comic, the tragedian, the villain, and so on. You and I are the directors within whose orbit the actors perform their various parts, some well, some poorly. We are, of course, the 'I's and take credit or blame for the totality of the performance, with special comments on some of the performers.

Time passes and the performers change. On the death of the Director they are affected by age, by the Black Cloud, by the Universal Mind. Some may shrink, or burn out. Some may just move into space like the millions of dead and living stars. Others may have been identified by the Mind of the Universe and steered in who knows what direction.

The actor who at some stage was ill-thought of and called Evil, may, like most of the others, have taken or been taken on any of these routes. S/he has started on a journey none can predict.

But evil? No.

Other states, other minds

Notes about places

I have been wondering what, if anything, to say about all the places written about briefly in the next few pages. They are connected with the ideas discussed in the rest of the book, but I was not sure how to define them. My problem is not an unusual one. It is to do with the relationship between the crowd and the individual member of the crowd; it concerns the single individual and her nature and her rights, and the population. It's about the extent to which that population, the many, can tolerate the idiosyncrasy of the quirky individual. Or in some cases, how much the population can put up with the whims of the leader, or of the leading group.

In the discussions on Emptiness with which the first parts of the book are mainly concerned, there was some speculation about how individual human beings may develop, becoming increasingly receptive to the Mind of the Universe. As they do so (we may perhaps dare to assume) they move beyond 'human affairs'. But it seems probable that human logic – for example, the sad traditional logic of war and violence – will survive to some extent in some cultures.

I had hoped originally to show the impact of the Black Cloud over a period of years by economic, medical, demographic and other criteria. I found, however, that there were so many variables, so many dubious criteria, that a full and honest analysis was beyond me. Instead I decided simply to indicate places in which it appears that unusually encouraging or grossly abnormal events had occurred during the period in which I was involved with them.

I decided to divide the rest of this section into two.

The first will be composed of brief notes on countries or parts of nations with which I have had dealings and which appear to have succumbed to the Black Cloud and suffered some extremely abnormal experiences or disaster, such as the massacres of Tutsis in Rwanda in 1994.

The second section consists of a selection of vignettes of various places of which I have had some close personal experience and which may suggest how events may unfold within a given setting. For example, take South Africa. I have not attempted to write about the major effect on society of the apartheid regime. But I have given a detailed account of my experience of it. I hope it may be helpful to the reader to trace the connection between the broad political or social picture and its implications for the individual human being.

Going (roughly) west to east from Ghana (in which we very happily lived), I begin with the principal Balkan states: Croatia, Serbia and Bosnia with Kosovo in a more ambiguous role. All of these committed, and suffered, acts of fearful harm and cruelty through the tangle of wars lasting a decade. But there was little to compare with the massacre in Srebrenica by Serb forces under Mladic (still not caught and brought to trial) of around 7,000 Bosnian men and boys, presumably to prevent them from joining the resistance. This stands out among many bestial episodes. I must say, however, that not long after, I met several Serb ex-soldiers who bitterly regretted this and other ghastly excesses. (Please note that the subsequent chapter named Osijek, a Croat town in the Balkans, has more to do with peace, to which one particular group has made a contribution of global significance.)

The next port of call is South Africa, where the astonishing transformation from the oppressive racist state to democracy took place with hardly any dissent. A former 'criminal', Nelson Mandela, became in a very short while, the president.

Mugabe, now president of Zimbabwe, was a respected leader of the Shona wing of the resistance movement, which he led from Mozambique. At the end of the war, however, he launched what might be termed a pre-emptive strike against his compatriot, but rival, group, the Ndebele. The troops he used for this task were the 5th Brigade, notorious for cruelty and violence. They killed 15,000 people.

Next the horrific massacres in Rwanda of the Tutsis by the Hutu tribe. They slew some 800,000 in a few weeks after a long period of coldly careful planning.

An account of Chitral, a remote settlement established by the Mongol empire under Tamurlane in Central Asia is included as an example of the continued existence of a pre-mediaeval 'culture', a model against which to assess modern society.

Pakistan and India are unhappily linked in my mind by the reciprocal escalation of violence between Muslim and Hindu at the time of partition. A great exchange took place by train between members of the two faiths – the Muslims going to Lahore, and the Hindus to Amritzar. At first all went smoothly. But then someone decided to cut off a foot. There followed a horrible period of escalating reciprocal amputation until there was nothing left to cut off. Decapitated Indians and Pakistanis silently shuttled back and forth between the grief-stricken families. And a tragic retake of this awful fanaticism took place much more recently when 2000 Muslims were slaughtered in Gujerat.

Bangladesh did not exist when I visited East Pakistan, as it then was, but I was very sad when I learned that the charming and talented Chakmas and the other Buddhists who had settled there centuries ago were being persecuted and driven out into Assam. We must realise that while any level of violence persists there can be no perfect peace. I do not just mean the violence of war, but the more subtle violence of word and particularly of thought, especially because it is silent.

Lastly I must mention Sri Lanka, thought of by western tourists as a peaceful paradise. Far from it. First, the Tamil war seeking independence from Colombo, and at last after twenty-five years, perhaps getting it. However there have also been two so-called JVP conflicts. These were most vicious struggles, fought between Buddhists. The aggressors in both cases have been young, mostly unemployed but educated young people. I lived through most of the second one and was shocked by its violence, desperation and great loss of life.

The aetiology of all these appears to me to have been understandable (if not justifiable), but the cruelty and ferocity certainly not. Any readers who study the next few sections, in which some of the situations and incidents are elaborated, may judge whether in so many cases the magnitude and ferocity of the wars was exacerbated by the Black Cloud.

There is of course much we can, and successfully, do to make a more peaceful world. And we should certainly enjoy life to the full, but we must never deceive ourselves that there is now nothing to worry about politically, medically, economically or, much more dangerously, believe that there is some intractable malfunctioning of the mind for which there is no specific remedy.

The truth is that the more peacefully and lovingly we live, the more we will help our neighbours to do the same. If we can bridge the gap between each other's communities, the more we will detoxify the poisons of fear and hatred, the more we will calm the miserable desperation of the Black Cloud, the closer will come the peace of the Universal Mind, and the sooner shall we be lost in its embrace.

But the truth is by no means always simple. The stories which follow are complex and various and an analysis of all the possibly relevant factors – social, economic, political, historical and so on – would be gigantic.

It seems to me reasonable, however, to adapt to communities, even very large ones, some of the same criteria that we apply to individuals. The supporters of a particular football team, political party, intellectual cult, fervent religious group, in fact the ardent supporters of any particular movement belief or theory or passion or faction – artistic, literary, sporting, intellectual, regional or whatever – lose to some extent their freedom. They commit acts of which they would never have dreamed themselves possible. The monstrous Hutus, the Hindu murderers of Gujerat, the Nazi concentration camp guards, brainwashed members of the Lord's Resistance Army, any of the millions of those who have committed obscene cruelties and earned the world's opprobrium, are victims of deprived and distorted minds and bodies.

They may have been victims of the Black Cloud in its various forms, or they may have been born and brought up in areas of corrupted social norms, or great social and economic poverty; in communities with very poor education or none.

The Mind of the Universe, from which we all derive and of which we all are part, has every gift needed to build a perfect being. We may take our choice. Mine, as I stated earlier, are Love, Compassion, Courage and Generosity. These and of course other gifts are whittled away by the Black Cloud and with obstinate frequency by its ally the Three Poisons. Hopefully, however, we are clear enough to retain a sufficient (but what is sufficient?) portion.

Then there is the insidious factor of 'propriety'. We cannot help recognizing that various attributes and qualities (e.g. love, courage, etc.) are considered good and as such admired. We may appear to have acquired these, and indeed really to have done so, but the Cockerel (see p2) will suss out the fraud and subtly spread the venom.

We all invest some of our feeling, though not necessarily much, on bogus virtue. I have no doubt, however, that there are many extreme examples of great intensity and powerful ego involvement which may be dangerously deceptive. These may be very gratifying. But I am not arguing that this powerful personal involvement is desirable.

The difference is that gifts from the Mind of the Universe are not cherished and developed for the benefit of the individual, who may develop these benefits, these gifts, at great cost to her strength, health, comfort, and lax enjoyment.

On the contrary, however, those men and women who are captured by even a small dose of one of the mildly tempting moral poisons are contributing to a possibly increasing tendency. *These in fact are the deadly poisons of the Self, of which Meister Eckhart was so keenly aware.* Or rather the tendency increases, because the satisfaction decreases, which is another way of saying that the need increases and the habit grows proportionately. And, of course, if the use of the habit does not increase, the desire, the need, grows – whether the habit is or for drugs or sex or adulation or political position.

But the more the need grows, the more 'human' it becomes, the further it slips away from the ultimate, the real growth of the Universal mind, until its inner being is utterly annihilated.

How does all this moralizing apply to the feelings, the states of mind of the nations to be considered – and of course to others?

In one sense we can only say that the 'moral standing' of any group is its own responsibility and that all leaders should consider these matters. But do they? Leaders can, however, and usually do, slough off moral responsibility.

The results are only too obvious in the places considered, with the possible exceptions of Chitral.

Ireland

My family and I returned to England in 1973 after having spent many years abroad – and Anne even longer. My new job was to set up a pioneering academic venture, Peace Studies, in the University of Bradford. At this time The Troubles in Northern Ireland were at their noisiest and I knew nothing about them. It would be disgraceful, I thought, if I didn't at least go there.

So I did. For the next four years I went on average every other weekend and for longer periods during vacation times with Anne. Our daughter Deborah was also hooked. She stayed with Irish friends, attended demonstrations and work camps, and once when I was watching the TV in Bradford I saw her bright cheerful face on the screen – there was some riot in Belfast, but she was quite merry.

I was completely confused by it all, but on taking stock at the end of a year of meetings, discussions, and listening in both Northern Ireland and Eire, I realised I was in the middle of the jungle and knew almost everyone in the higher echelons of the IRA and the Protestant paramilitary organisations – and liked them all very much. I met only a few of the political leaders, but nobody thought much of them and they had much less influence than the fighters. I liked and respected most of the clergy I met: and the two bishops, Catholic and Church of England, whom I got to know, were splendid. It was tragic that all these brave, tough and intelligent men (not the clergy) were hell bent on killing each other.

After a couple of years I met a man called Joe. He made his money by repairing electrical goods such as refrigerators, televisions and radios. But his driving force was a passionate longing to resolve the problems of Ireland. He believed the fighters of the various private armies should lay aside their political disagreements and work together for matters of common community concern – housing, public services, schools, transportation, health. Joe was convinced that the effort and the energy, let alone the absence of completely unproductive conflict, would work wonders if transferred from the unproductive struggle. The first step, he believed strongly, would be to bring together fairly senior representatives to discuss these issues jointly.

He worked with passionate intensity on members of all the major militant groups, and miraculously they all agreed to attend a meeting. They also agreed not to bring their guns.

We were to meet in a small hotel in a remote part of the Donegal mountains in Eire. About twenty-five people came. They were not the generals, as it were, but the colonels. This meant that the top brass were tentatively in favour at least of exploring Joe's idea.

The men arrived (no women, of course). Their manner was guarded but civil. I was reminded of dogs meeting each other for the first time, walking stiffly round each other, ready to spring if the other made a suspicious movement.

Actually, as well as serious talking, there was a lot of singing and it was a delight to watch an IRA member and one from the UDA (Ulster Defence Association) clasped together and singing a duet. These were men who may have lived only a street away, but had never actually seen each other except through the sights of an Armalite rifle. Now, however, several men of both faiths said to me confidentially, 'Do you know, those – Catholics, or Protestants – are really pretty nice.'

An interesting thing happened on the way back to Northern Ireland. One of the more senior Protestants had trouble with his car, which kept stopping. The last time it did so was just a few yards from a dangerous stretch of road, very steep, winding, and with an unprotected precipitous declivity on the left. I had come up that way en route for the hotel, and recognised its dangers.

A following car full of IRA members, one of whom was a good mechanic, fixed the trouble. The third time, however, he realised that the trouble was more radical than he had thought. But he located and corrected the fault. The driver thanked him, set off down the hill, and eventually arrived safely home.

One of the IRA men said to me later, 'Thank God he stopped where he did. If the engine had stalled just a few yards further on he was bound to have been killed. But no one would have believed it was an accident. His lot would have made war on the IRA and we would never have been trusted again.'

Another meeting was held in Holland, but I was not involved. Sadly, it was disastrous. Some of the press were there and there was none of the peaceful camaraderie we had enjoyed in Donegal. We had not, it is true, come up with any startling declarations, still less with a plan. But we had laid the foundations of a relationship which could have borne more specific fruit.

The Northern Ireland Secretary had kept a distant but not unfriendly eye on Joe's ideas. However, he was promoted to Home Secretary and an entirely unsuitable man appointed, hasty, irascible, insensitive, give-them-a-sharp-lesson theorist without discovering what had already happened. Muddle and confusion took over, people were killed mysteriously.

Things became very difficult for Joe and he went through a bad time. I am glad to say, however, that he overcame his difficulties and did work which rightly earned him an honorary doctorate for some very valuable mediation carried out far from Ireland.

So far, I have never returned to Ireland, a country whose two portions I love greatly despite their extraordinary ability to irritate.

Nigeria

After nearly three years in Ghana, we had something of a toe-hold in Africa, including a minor contact in Nigeria where a colleague had set up a research project. I enjoyed going there greatly.

Early in 1966, however, it seemed horridly probable that there would be actual war between the mediaeval and Muslim northern and the predominantly Christian western Nigeria. The British had done a deal with the north. The monarchical northern emirs had agreed to maintain law and order and to collect taxes, if the British would refrain from instituting either missionary work, or non-Muslim education. Northern Nigeria remained a feudal and autocratic, under-developed region very dependent on skilled and educated products of largely Christian schools and colleges. By the time I knew anything about Nigeria there was much tension and a serious increase of violence.

Another factor was oil. The great preponderance of the oil-rich area was in the western region, which embittered the much poorer north and made the people of the western region irritatingly smug vis à vis the north. At the time when I was becoming concerned about the situation the governance of the country was shaky, the prime minister was assassinated, and a young colonel (then general) selected instead, Yakobu Gowon. He was a northerner, a point of satisfaction to most parties, but also a Christian from the middle belt, an area dominated by small tribes rather than the very predominant Hausa Fulani of the north. His opposite number was Colonel Chukwu Emeka Odumegwu Ojukwu, once an army colleague with the Federal leader, with whom he had actually shared a flat.

Two of us were sponsored by the Quakers to study what seemed likely to burst into flames. John Volkmar was designated to visit Nigeria in the spring of 1967 and report back to the Quakers (though their attention was somewhat diverted by the outbreak of the Seven Days War). I was to accompany him.

We came back pessimistic. What put the lid on it, for me at least, was an afternoon with a most gentle and devout Christian minister, also a physician, who had held high office in the United Nations. A peace advocate if anyone was! While we were talking with him someone brought the news that five young Biafrans (this new name for the people of the western region was by now semi-official) had kidnapped some planes of the Nigerian Air Lines and flown them into the now capital of Biafra, Owerri. On hearing this news our elderly host jumped up and down shouting with joy. This, I was certain, meant that war was almost inevitable. It started in a few months with a successful Biafran drive towards the capital. But the army, though well trained and efficient, was too small to maintain an advance so far from its base. The main war was fought, a slow, lethal slog down from the north through the jungle. And the slow and even more lethal starvation of the Biafran people developed into a ghastly famine. But there seemed to be no place for us at the beginning, and we did not become directly involved for the first months of a three-year conflict. The reason was that none of the leaders wanted outsiders who were interested in peace.

Some months after the beginning of war, however, John, whose work took him all over West Africa, had a meeting with Hamani Diore, president of Niger, who advised him that the time was ripe for a pacific approach to the warring parties, which had previously been rejected. We went therefore to Lagos, then the capital.

At first we had great trouble: there was only one fairly senior civil servant on the Federal side who was helpful in a limited fashion. However, to get to Biafra, officially a deviant part of Federal Nigeria, we needed the permission of the head of state, General Yakobu Gowon. But we couldn't get an appointment to meet him. A certain Mr Black, through whom all requests had to pass, firmly and repeatedly said 'No'. (As it happened, we did later meet Mr Black. He turned out to be a most delightful man and a good friend who was only concerned to spare the general unnecessary trouble.) Eventually, however, we met the head of the foreign ministry who thought it might be helpful for us to meet the head of state.

General Gowon had not wanted to see us because he had had bad experiences with intrusive journalists. These, he said, had ruined a potentially constructive meeting in Ghana, and he didn't want another débacle. But he then hastened to say that he was glad to see representatives of the Quakers.

We told him that one of our people in Geneva had spoken to the Austrian Chancellor about our concern for a locale for a meeting on the conflict. He had then promised to lend us a remote castle where we could meet without any unwanted visitors.

But rightly, I think, the general said he thought it would be too far away, but that he wanted to be in touch with any debates or proposals.

We then said that we would appreciate a visit to the rebels (as we had been advised to call them). We said we would be happy to discuss with Ojukwu anything which might facilitate the quest for peace.

The general did not disapprove, but told us we must make it clear to Colonel Ojukwu that he would accept no compromise; he was in rebellion and must face the consequences of his illegal actions and the devastation and deaths he had caused.

He then went on to say he hoped very much that our journey would be safe. But he also warned us that we would be flying in an illegal plane and that his war planes had instructions to destroy any 'pirates'. He hoped, he said, that we would not be shot down, but that it would be impossible to pick out particular planes, especially at night.

We said we understood the dangers and, having been under fire before, were quite prepared to accept the risk.

He finally said that if we got back safely he would be glad if we would come to see him and his give him our impressions of how things were on the other side.

After this we returned to London where there was a long, boring wait. It transpired that Ojukwu was waiting until he had collected a cross-section of clergy, including an archbishop (and us). The journey was tiresome. We began by being taken to a remote corner of Lisbon Airport (the whole operation was very clandestine) where we boarded a ramshackle old plane having a few rows of seats in front and piles of military material crammed into the rest of the plane's belly.

Eventually we set off and chugged down the African coast until we reached Portuguese Guinea, where we stopped for a most welcome bacon and egg breakfast. At this stage in the slow liberation of the colonies, no Portuguese planes were allowed to overfly the African coast line. Then, nourished, we turned left as darkness fell and headed landwards above the mangrove swamps to the Biafran town of Port Harcourt. The lights and radio which might have guided the Nigerian war planes towards us were switched off. But the pilot turned back and flew out to sea again. He said he had been off course and feared that with his own radio turned off he might have been lured by the Nigerian air force station to within the range of its anti-aircraft fire.

So back we flew back to the island of Sao Tome, another tiny speck of Portuguese territory, one which like Guinea Bissau is now a pigmy independent republic.

But the next evening we made landfall successfully. We were lodged in an otherwise empty hotel and given the sumptuous dinner we should have had the night before. I could scarcely bear to eat those by then almost extinct delicacies.

I never went there again; it was overrun by the Nigerian army soon after. And I never had such an easy landing. The next time the pilot had to do without lights and land on a widened road, covered with leaves during daylight to disguise it from the questing war planes. The last time, the Nigerian pilots had located it; a friend of mine, a priest who helped out running the 'air port', was wounded by a Nigerian bomb. A few years before he had been interrogated by a group of Biafran fighters. When they asked him what work he did, he replied that he was a missionary. They thought he said he was a mercenary (there were some unpleasant examples of these) and tortured him, breaking all the fingers of one hand. Then they expelled him from the country and said if he returned he would be killed. But here he was again, in great danger of both bombs and the fighters who had tortured him. And his heroism extended to lending me his bed.

Our task in Biafra, as indeed in the 'legitimate' area of the country, was to explore the possibility of peace initiatives, or to suggest tentatively ways of overcoming obstacles to a ceasefire (or indeed slight relaxing of the implacably obstinate repetition of the hard line both sides adopted).

I should comment here that conflicts in the 1960s and '70s were in some ways more narrowly inflexible than those in the '80s and after, by when most wars had become very much internationalised and the diplomacy more complex. But the issue of oil in Nigeria was already complicating tribal rivalry.

What happened in Nigeria, however, is relatively minor compared with the decade of horror in the Congo basin. Two major types of conflict tore the region apart. One was the influx of Hutu brought under eventual control after their orgy of butchery in Rwanda, and then freed to inflict their savagery unchecked in the Congo region. The other, of course, was that six other African countries contested with each other like vultures for the pickings of mineral-rich areas. The scale of the Congo bestiality exceeded even the awful Biafran famine in which nearly a million, particularly children, starved to death.

I remember one particularly moving incident. I was walking down a jungle trail when I met a group of women going the other way. And with surprise I saw among them a Biafran woman friend I had met in happier days. We embraced weeping. I gave her all the medicines I had (there were now none left in Biafra) but we had to hurry on our different ways and parted almost immediately. I had no time even to ask after her family. I never found out if her children were still alive.

Our job was, of course, to get into touch with the leaders. It was not very easy in such chaotically violent circumstances, but we caught up with Ojukwu in his jungle headquarters. He was an impressively powerful and eloquent character.

'I usually have a cup of coffee at this time of day,' he said with the air of having nothing else to do. 'Will you join me?'

We did. Ojukwu stuck me as able, ruthless and self-seeking. If he had been less autocratically ambitious, he could have carved out for himself a strong and nationally useful position in a united Nigeria. Instead he was largely responsible for a terrible toll of death and misery.

On the other side most of the leading Biafrans were outstanding human beings. Two, who were particular friends, had both been heads of universities. One told me he had been offered a chair at Harvard and was sad that he couldn't accept it. We did however meet there after the war, but unfortunately he died very soon. Another Biafran academic, well-known for his wonderful writing, was Chinua Achebe who has now lived some time in the USA. I travelled with him once in one of the 'pirate' planes, as General Gowon called them. These and other Biafrans were the cream of Nigerian intellectuals. They said that being the Christian minority of the country, the various educational bodies had done their best to redress the balance. They had been successful, but had created an elite that supported and helped plan the war, and the imbalance in the northern economy that precipitated the war. But the leaders formed a clique of ambitious, sophisticated and entertaining intelligentsia. I much enjoyed their company on the many plane journeys together to conferences set up by the UN, the Organisation of African Unity and other bodies in London, Paris, Addis Ababa, Algeria, Kampala etc. concerned by the conflict. Busy meetings with fruitless outcomes – the murderous killing continued.

Time passed.

For me there was one very significant but mostly unnoticed chain of events. At one stage I was taken to a place of great sorrow. I was told that one hundred and twenty-eight market women, mostly with babies on their backs, had been killed by a single cluster bomb.

The Biafran conducting me said that the plane came in flying very low, dropped its bomb, and sped away. It is worth noting that at this stage the Nigerian army was hiring Egyptian pilots who were flying Russian Migs, a fallible arrangement.

Making no attempt to gloss over this ghastly happening, I said it was just possible that this was an inexperienced pilot making his getaway as fast as possible, going too fast to spot the market and the women and just wanting to get rid of his bombs anywhere.

But my Biafran friend would have nothing of this.

'No,' he said. 'It's just on a par with everything else: genocide. They want to wipe us like insects off the face of the earth and claim the oil and everything else. They are jealous of us; they know we are much smarter than them and now they think they've got a good chance of getting rid of us all. Bastards!'

I was determined to talk to Gowon about this and as soon as possible I started on the awkward journey. The unpredictable plane from the Uli airstrip in the forest, the flight via Sao Tome to Lisbon, change, then on to Heathrow. Then the reverse and more simple flight down to Lagos.

This time there was no delay about getting to see the Commander-in-Chief.

I told him the story and he expressed a grief which I am sure was completely open and genuine.

'It's tragic,' he said. 'But although these people are rebels, they are truly my people. All they have to do is to lay down their arms and give up their rebellion.'

I answered that they been told this, and simply did not believe it. They believed his offers of amnesty and pardon were simply a trick to make them give up the struggle, so that he could slaughter them more easily, and that the episode of the bombing was just an example of his treacherous malevolence.

I added that in my opinion killing and defeating an enemy may force an end to fighting, but not bring peace. On the contrary, hatred will fester, and one day the slaughter will start again. He looked very sad. He sighed and said, 'Yes, I see.'

Time passed.

I was in London with my family on sabbatical leave from Harvard. Early one morning I had a phone call from the Commonwealth Secretary General, who said he had just got the surprising news that the war was rapidly coming to an end as the Biafran army was collapsing. This was a great surprise: everyone had expected it would go on fighting for about another six months. Nothing, therefore, had been done to prepare for what might be a chaotic situation. In particular there was likely to be a massacre of their defeated enemies by the victorious Federal forces. The SG then said that as I knew the leadership on both sides I might be able to do something to mitigate the probable disaster. I agreed to do my best, but with great misgivings. I had a hopeless vision of standing between two armies like a traffic cop – and being run over by both sides.

But all my prognostications were wrong. Firstly, by the time I reached Lagos, the war was over. But not with a bloodbath. The Federal army soldiers treated their defeated enemies like brothers. They gave them their own rations, took them to feeding centres or to hospital if needed. One of the most senior Biafrans was actually staying in my hotel, going around and talking to old friends he had not seen for the nearly three years of war.

As for me, I felt blissfully happy; the horrors of the bombing of the market were being wonderfully replaced. Going back in my mind, I recalled my talk with General Gowon and wondered how this fine young soldier had achieved this miraculous transformation of a notoriously ruthless army.

South Africa (apartheid)

We are now beginning a completely different sort of intellectual journey. To start with, we were travelling through the intricacies and mysteries of Mind. Now our journeys are bodily. The pronoun 'we' stands for my wife Anne, our year-old baby Deborah and my mother, aged a lively 80.

It came about like this. Earlier in the year, the president of Ghana, Kwame Nkrumah, announced that the whole of the economics department of the

University of Ghana (in which I was a professor) would be dismissed because they were incompetent and not up-to-date in their economics. Moreover, it was hinted also that they were politically offensive to the left-wing president.

All this led to great excitement. Meetings were held and passionate orations delivered. I am ashamed to say that I spoke loudly about 'the company of scholars' and became very popular for a while. But I also greatly regretted the whole shermozzle. I liked Nkrumah and agreed with most of his ideas. When we met, however, we talked more about our babies, born the same weekend, than about politics. But I was influenced by another possible future. I had been offered a visiting professorship at Harvard and though it was only for a year, I was buoyantly convinced that something desirable would turn up afterwards. In addition, I had been invited to go to Bhutan as an advisor. (In the end this fell through. The Bhutan authorities said that the ten-day journey to the capital might be too much for a young baby. This was a pity as it would have been a unique chance to see the country before it was opened up.)

But there was something more important.

At that time (1959-61) there were very few English-type universities in Africa, and we in the West would exchange visits with one in Uganda from time to time. But also at that 'less developed' era it was only possible to fly via South Africa. So I would fly to Johannesburg, spend the night, and then proceed next day to the university at Makerare, our sister institution.

Let me return briefly to Ghana. One of my best friends there was a South African refugee, Leslie Rubin. He was a lawyer and had been one of the four senators to represent the black population. He was so radically opposed to the apartheid regime that he had to escape and continued his work against the South African government partly through friends who remained in the country, and made use of legitimate travellers like me as couriers. During my short visits to Johannesburg I made contact with one of his good friends, also a lawyer, called John. I passed on the papers Leslie had given me for him, and John gave me in return much more information than was wise. John, as you will see, was reckless about himself – and in fact, about others. But for the time being he spun his web of intrigue and wove me, and therefore my little family, into it.

During one short visit to South Africa I raised an issue which became extremely important to me and a number of other people. Black Africans had been excluded to some extent from 'white' higher education. Steps were now being taken to extend the ban to all Black students, except for a very small number of very special courses. I decided that if I became in any sense involved actively in South Africa, it should be to set up some sort of higher educational organisation, if not actually in the country, in one of the small satellite nations like Swaziland.

Soon afterwards I returned to Ghana, having made what turned out to be my last trip to Makerere – but not to Johannesburg. One day I got a message to say that a friend had arrived at the airport and wanted to talk to me. John.

Ghana was at that time the only independent sub-Saharan country and deeply detested by South Africa, both for its politics and as a haven for hostile refugees. If it were known that John had come to Ghana illicitly, he would be in vast trouble.

I took him to see some of my friends, ending up with the finance minister who promised him £20,000. This would be very helpful in many ways – for example, enabling John himself to escape not very long after. This visit delighted me greatly: I was, however, slightly worried lest he would find it hard not to reveal something, some tiny hint about his visit to Ghana. He did not, in fact, do so – but did something equally dangerous for us.

The few days (or perhaps weeks) before our departure were desperate. A very sad thing was that one of my students, driven by another, died in a tragically absurd accident crossing nothing much more than a rickety bridge over a stream. The funeral was tragically awful. The academics sweltered in their gowns, the sixth form in their smart black suits sang, 'Play up, play up and play the game', and what we call a witch doctor in full regalia, shaking, crouching and dancing, weaved round the crowd.

Anne passed out from heat and the exhaustion of preparation to leave at a dinner given by some young Turks (non-political ones); I suffered with a kidney stone; while my mother and Deborah, the very old and the very young, were fine.

Our caravan probably looked both ridiculous and brave as we set out, cluttered with all the lumber of the little household. Our friends waved, dubiously hopeful, as we set out for an unknown journey which we guessed could be unpleasant. All our large and solid stuff had already gone into the plane's belly and we struggled across the tarmac and up the stairway with saucepans, wicker basket filled with baby odds and ends, and heavy coats (we were going into winter).

We settled down quite contentedly on the plane. After some time I looked down through the darkening sky to the remote and terribly alien waters of the Okavengo swamp. I suddenly felt a frisson of fear. But it wasn't too long before we were being greeted by John and his wife Brenda, a brave and charming woman. She welcomed us with wonderful warmth into their home.

Nothing much happened for a day or two, except a party at which we met Alan Paton, the conscience and great writer of South Africa. I was keen to have the chance to discuss the university project, as my mind referred to it.

Then, on the third night in South Africa, I was shaken awake roughly. A large, dim figure loomed above me. 'Get up quickly,' he said. 'Colonel Spengler wants to talk to you.'

I had already heard much about this man. He had a reputation for ruthless brutality, but boasted that he had only killed one man by hand, as he usually let his underlings finish the job. He was the policeman responsible for the notorious massacre, in which I think 79 people died. And here he was, sitting in John and Brenda's main living room. His first words were, 'We know how to make you talk.'

I thought that this was probably true, but was determined not to let him know.

The interrogation went on for several hours. It was based on a letter which John had apparently written and given to a Swazi prince who was searched at Jan Smuts airport. It contained such phrases as, 'Adam Curle's visit will give us great encouragement to carry out the project you know about'.

'What is this project?' shouted Spengler, whose first name was appropriately 'Attila'; his friends called him Utt as it sounded in Afrikaans.

I said truthfully that I didn't know, at least not in any detail, but I was very interested. Spengler grunted angrily and then changed to the good-cop-bad-cop routine. 'Major Lamprecht,' he said, 'you knock some sense into this man. I'm getting angry and you know what I do then.'

'No, no, Colonel,' said Lamprecht, 'Don't talk like that. He's an educated man. Just talk to him good and he will be helpful to us – because he's an educated man.' He then said he would like to take me on a tour of the country and I would see how happy everyone was and how well the natives were treated – and anyway, how much they all loved the Queen. This went on for about five hours, during a part of which they were having a go at John. This had happened before and John had been charged, but acquitted by the courts (which had not been corrupted as they later were). With the proceeds of his compensation, John had bought this house, which was consequently known as Spengler's Folly. But behind the buffoonery Spengler was venomous. He was also very abnormal. Extremely brutal with men, he was terrified of women. Brenda knew that he would never venture into a place where women were likely to go, and so used the kitchen as a safe. She kept her confidential papers there and hid her passport in a saucepan. (Some time later in the month-long interrogation, I had a recurrence of my kidney trouble and once when Anne came to visit me in hospital, she found him just about to start questioning me. She flew at him like a tigress protecting her cub. 'What the hell are you doing here: get out, get out!' she shouted. He scuttled off immediately, gibbering.

Towards dawn Spengler left with his entourage, apart from one policeman as a guard, John and Brenda, Anne and I got together to consider what to do.

John, however, felt he had no options. He said, 'It's no good. They've got me. They'll search the office – at it now perhaps – and they'll find all the evidence to put me away for a very long time. So I'm off now, as soon as I can.' A bit later he was flown to Zimbabwe, at that stage still Rhodesia possibly. We gave him all the ready cash we had (I'd only got £30.) He got out of a window at the back of the house, scrambled down the steep wooded hill, and to the housing block where they had a flat to be used for such occasions. A friend had been called to bring a car, in which they drove immediately to Swaziland (there had not been time to set up road blocks) and thence, without any trouble, to Salisbury (later Harare) and on to London where we eventually met again with Leslie Rubin.

This was a rude start. We didn't have an idea how to get going on our new project. But there was one immediate problem: how to deal with our personal predicament. Spengler and his gang would be on to me first thing next morning –

in fact in a couple of hours! I was then whisked off to the notorious Greys to continue the grilling

The fairly obvious first step would be for Anne or me to contact the UK embassy and hope they would get actively into the game. But if they were unhelpful, casting me as a tiresome lefty with American connections, it could be positively unrewarding; the South African government would not be exercising any restraint, as it now seemed to be doing. I decided on balance not to appeal to the embassy.

Instead I resolved to rubbish their attempts to substantiate their case against me, confusing and deceiving them. For example, on one occasion they read me a letter that they had intercepted. It was from a friend, but not a very close one. In this he mentioned someone with the same name as a rather notorious left-wing politician. Lamprecht proceeded to quiz me about this politician. I then led him on with more or less fictitious stories both inflammatory and defamatory about this poor fellow. All this must have sounded highly suspicious to a good (old style) South African. At last he burst out with an excited question. 'Where is this fellow now? I'd like to ask him a few questions.'

'I'm sorry to say, Major, that he passed away five years ago.'

Lamprecht spluttered furiously. 'Why are you telling me all this crap?'

'Well, you asked me questions and I answered truthfully. Just read his biography and you'll see.'

'Sorry,' he muttered. And he continued the session, but taking a different line: the wickedness of unbelievers and scoffers of true religion. However I knew enough of the Bible to be able to correct occasional misquotations. Thereafter he treated me with greater respect and caution.

Over several days my slightly firmer, even aggressive, manner somewhat modified the manner of both my interrogators. This encouraged me to take a further step. I told them that I knew they had a difficult job, and had tried not to make it harder by protesting to my embassy. But now, I said, I had had enough. And I wanted to be free to leave the country without any adverse comments from them.

This was very important, because during this period the South African authorities had an unpleasant habit of making statements that the reason why people were expelled was because they were communists. If this were to happen to us, because the USA were equally fastidious I might be refused entry to the USA – and not be able to take up my Harvard job.

But I strengthened my position by evoking my American contacts. I told them that David Bell was a great friend of mine. And explained that he was President Kennedy's director of the budget, and of course largely responsible for overseas aid, much needed now that official links with the UK had been broken.

I think this may well have been true because with surprising speed the minister was telephoned, the passports were returned, and a kindly lawyer friend of John's – though not part of his 'gang' of conspirators – was seeing us off safely on the plane for England (via Rhodesia, then of course, a British colony). We arrived to shelter and subdued but tasteful luxury with my cousin Ursula. It was wonderful to be both comfortable and safe.

After a few days, however, Ursula said, 'I keep on seeing this odd little man, the one in the bubble car and flowered shirt.'

But Anne was unexpectedly alarmed. 'Please tell me if you see him again.'

And a few minutes later, she did. He was going down the other side of the street.

Anne rushed to the window and returned looking oddly shocked. 'It's him,' she said. 'It's Spengler disguised as a tourist.'

It seemed like some horrible magic. He was spying on us obviously, but how on earth had he discovered us? Then I remembered, he had shown me a letter he had intercepted, just given me a glimpse of the address, to scare me with his apparently magical power.

I phoned Leslie, who had arrived in London a few days before. He happened to be a friend of the Home Secretary, who immediately asked him to come round. John, who had arrived (with the help of the plane bought with Ghanaian cash!), went with him. But I thought it better to stay with Anne and the baby.

The Home Secretary was surprised, indignant and slightly amused at the unpleasant cop in the bubble car. 'Well, well,' he said. 'We can't have that sort of thing going on.'

We were amused to hear, a few says later, that Johannesburg papers had reported Spengler's rapid round trip. He had returned the same day that Anne saw him.

I felt much relieved. As soon as I heard he was in London, despite the absurdity of the little bubble car, I felt a crawling horrid fear, more than when I had actually been dealing with him. I now imagined myself walking peacefully somewhere in London, unaware that Spengler's goon was about to creep up silently, spring on me, clap a pad of chloroform over my face, bundle me into the back of a van, fly me off to Johannesburg and the Grays, which I knew all too well, and from which I would never emerge.

I chided myself as paranoid until I heard, a few years later, that Spengler's next job had been to arrange the kidnapping of 'wanted' people from countries outside South Africa. Some of his victims I had known.

Much later in England I also met some of John's lot of brave if rash conspirators. One, who became a colleague of mind, had been imprisoned for ten years.

Chitral

The uphill slog was somewhat tedious, apart from the cheerful stream beside us with its garnish of little purple flowers. But then we were on the lovely level plane of the Shandur Pass. A gleaming lake lay over to the left and a mob of rather sedate dzos wandered round the edges. But the pleasant pass came to an end. The path lay before us, swooping and slithering down to the minute village far below. As we approached, we saw how low the houses were (at 10,000 feet the winter is arctic and it wasn't much better then) and there was little fuel beyond dry scrub. Looming over everything is Buni Zom, abrupt and menacing, but a relative teenager among the giants of the Pamir Knot at, I think, only 21,000 feet.

But we managed to have a cheerful evening, jam-packed together with our generous hosts. They brought some eggs as well as the fuel, and we had cigarettes to pass around (I smoked then) and some powdered soup from Kashgar, which was fairly horrible. We somehow managed to communicate with a jumble of words from different languages.

They told us about their life. They did a little farming, but couldn't grow much – the valley was too high. Anyway, the overlord in the castle we were going to next day levied a tax, which left them with hardly anything. The summer was always a season of famine when they had used up all they had of last year's crop and before this year's was ready.

'So what happened then?'
'We ate grass.'
'Was that any good at all?'
'Not much. Some of the old and the young died of hunger. Others died because the grass somehow tied itself into knots inside.'
'Don't the overlords help?'

This question was hardly worth answering. We didn't understand, they said politely, that they were different from us. They had come here, they said, so long ago, in the times of ignorance. They took charge of everything – the crops, the roads, everything. They told us what to do and we did it. That was best. There was a general murmur, but Anne and I were not quite sure what it signified. Perhaps they didn't all agree; perhaps they did. At least they seemed to react to our horrified response to what we were being told.

We set off very early next day. The overlord's castle was a long way away, but we didn't know how news of our imminent arrival had been sent. For several hours we walked down a narrow valley, getting very wet as we forded several large streams. At length the valley widened out and we could see far ahead the massive walls of the castle.

We were greeted by a castle official of some rank, who took us in to see the master. But he, the Colonel, was away in the state capital of Chitral. His rank followed the tradition of the scions of tribal chiefs training in India or even Sandhurst to wage war against other local rulers.

So here was this boy of perhaps twenty, and dressed as for an afternoon's tennis at Wimbledon. We sat together in the abundant orchard – also within the castle walls. There we had, as appearances had led us to expect, a very correct conversation. After that we were shown to our bedroom to prepare for dinner.

The boy's preparation, however, was very different from ours. He was dressed as a tribal chief, no truckling to the Brits. He began with the more savoury of the evening's entertainments. His great great etc. grandfather had ridden and fought with Tamurlane who, in gratitude for his loyalty, had given him this province, famed for the beauty of its women. Here the boy lapsed lyrical and licentious. Particularly the latter.

It became clear, however, that he preferred, if there were a choice, cruelty to carnality.

He spewed out a series of revolting stories of the atrocities carried out by his forbears. He told, for example, about how his grandfather had suspended his brother, aunt, grandson (it was best not to recall the details) over a fire which he gradually built up until the wretched creatures' shrieks and writhing were ended. Every so often he would say with great satisfaction, 'We are a bloody people.'

We left as early as we could, reminding him that, on his advice indeed, we were to leave at five in the morning.

And at five we were up and ready to make a move. We went outside the castle walls as we had been instructed, prepared to set off. No one was there. We went back to see if breakfast had been readied in the dining room. No, it hadn't. We went out again. Eventually the boy appeared looking sombre and remote.

We politely reminded him that he had arranged to meet us with horses at five. He replied brusquely that there weren't any horses. In fact I could see several in a small field just to the left of where we were standing. He looked at me sourly and walked away.

Some time later he reappeared with a group of about twenty men. They were wearing some sort of ragged uniform and were armed with swords. The boy was grinning and laughing with them, apparently giving them some instructions. He pointed at us and said something. They drew their weapons, looking a little worried.

Anne said to me, 'He's telling them to kill us. Shout angrily at him like a colonel.' So I did, finding it embarrassing but worried about what might happen if I didn't. I said, as loudly and fiercely as I could: 'Look here you young idiot, get those bloody horses organised, or it will be the worse for you.'

And it worked immediately and amazingly well. With the help of the soldiers, relieved not to have to kill us, we were saddled up, and away in a few minutes. The boy had somewhat recovered his nerve and rode along with us, a fine horseman, obviously, as is Anne; she would ride along the narrow path, nonchalantly chewing an apple, and with one leg overhanging a thousand foot drop. I would prefer to walk, except on a good level surface. I was not encouraged by Anne telling me she could see a body like a squashed plum at the bottom of the ravine.

Anyway, just as we were starting, the wretched lad rode up behind and cut my horse on the withers with his whip. He no doubt expected I would fall as my horse reacted, but although the good animal certainly did react, it was not enough to throw me.

Well, the next three days passed without very serious events. Poor Anne developed cystitis and we polished off the remains of our bottle of gin for its restorative qualities, as we bedded down in our sleeping bags in a rather rough little ravine. And several people were very nice to us

After three days we got to Chitral. A nice little town overhung by its vast 25,000 foot peak, the pride of the Hindu Kush. The Political Agent arranged for us to be put up in the school, which was much better than we had had for some days and Anne was beginning to improve considerably, but there was no gin to be had. Actually the PA was in a bad way. He had had a nasty crack on the head playing polo and had to retire to bed after coping with us.

The most interesting thing to happen before we returned over the passes to the semi-civilization of Swat was a meeting with the Colonel Khuswaqt, the father of Humayun, our young host. The colonel was a compact and formidable man of about fifty. He was staying in the local castle for a meeting of the Regency Council of the King, who was a little boy of six.

We told him we had been in his area of Chitral (he was the governor of the Northern Province). He said he was very sorry not to have been around to give us hospitality.

We said that we were sorry too, but that his son had looked after us well. He looked very startled.

'Was it ... ,' he said and paused anxiously. 'Was it all right?'

'Yes, it was fine,' we said.

He gave a deep breath. 'Well,' he said. 'I'm really very glad.'

What else could we have told him?

Zimbabwe

The Quakers had been deeply involved with Rhodesia (later Zimbabwe) for a number of years before I got embroiled with the country. This was soon after the débacle in Ireland. Walter Martin, a great Africanist with whom I had worked in Nigeria, was in charge of Quaker Peace Service. He asked if I would accompany him on a mission to Rhodesia/Zimbabwe and I agreed.

As is well known there was a bitter war going on in the country: the African population struggling for independence and the whites, of course, struggling to stave off what they thought to be disaster. The leader of the non-violent black Rhodesian movement, Bishop Muzorewa, was a crafty politician who did not utterly reject violence if convenient – but at the time when we went there, it wasn't. And there were two other black political parties.

The recognised leader of the Black violent resistance movement was Robert Mugabe, a Shona, who was based with his staff in Mozambique. His junior partner was Joshua Nkomo, who with his followers was an Ndebele. He and his staff were based in Zambia (where we also had the pleasure of meeting President Kenneth Kaunda who gave us some of the interesting books he had written). I also had the delight of meeting a great friend and former student, Trevor Coombe, a South African to whom the authorities in Zambia had given a Zambian passport, because they appreciated him and knew that he would be in trouble if he returned home. (I grieve that not too long ago KK, as he is known, was deposed for no clear reason.)

Walter and I did a lot of travelling. We felt it was important to keep in touch with the members of the Front Line States committee – Botswana, Mozambique, Zambia and Tanzania – where the chair, President Julius Nyerere, gave us good advice. South Africa was not, of course, in favour with 'rebellious' freedom fighters! However, the South Africans were a part of the jigsaw. I did actually have to go through South Africa – a few hours tedious wait until the next plane to what was still Rhodesia. I was always glad to board it, although the Foreign Office had been told that I would not be rearrested after my 'earlier troubles' if located at Jan Smuts (the airport named after the man who, I was told, had kissed me as a baby!).

Not very long after our first few somewhat inconclusive visits, the UK and (still) Rhodesia, with its several (black) political parties, were still teetering on the edge of dealing with the basic issues of independence. There was a lot of wangling at Clarence House in which I was only able to play a very small part, but it made a considerable impression on me. It had been agreed that both armies should withdraw to supervised camps. The Rhodesians had an ample number of barracks and properties of one sort or another, but the Zimbabwe forces did not, and were to be confined to, I think, twelve locations. But the representative of one of the political parties protested that they would be in danger – not from the Brits, but from the private army of another of the Zimbabwean armies. He argued that the previous year this rival of his had generously offered to provide new boots (or uniforms; I forget which) if the men were to collect in a particular spot. This offer was gratefully accepted. The rival, having more military clout, then sent in the helicopter gunships, killing most of them. The Brits, recognising this danger, then slightly increased the number of camps.

After infinite argy-bargy a deal was stuck. Rhodesia was handed over to Britain, and a governor in the large shape of Lord Soames (as I think he probably was then) took office. By no means everything was settled, but the main thing was that the country had given up the claim of independence.

Anne and I were already there, having been installed – as what, as I now wonder? Perhaps just as observers, But as subsequently became apparent, some things were not supposed to be observed.

The official programme was that after a given period, elections would be held. The victor would then take over and the British regime would take off.

The first step taken by the government, helped of course by the new Zimbabweans, was to take control of border crossings; after all, no one wanted undesirable aliens or mischief makers to confuse the delicate political balance. This meant none of the Patriotic Front, especially Mugabe. Packages of notepaper with 'Zimbabwe' headings should, for example, be destroyed or held up until after the election. The South Africans were also very helpful at this stage. For example, quite a number of troops were deployed on the frontier or even over it into Zimbabwe, to control any undemocratic incursions or demonstrations.

However, the government came to believe that it would be judicious to relax these restrictions somewhat. Even Mugabe was permitted entry. But he was considered a dangerous communist and there was evidence that communists had been active in attacking churches, which of course were not only places of worship but symbols of law and order, indeed of democracy. This was proved when churches were dynamited, though the evidence was somewhat confused: in one case the limbs of white men were found among the wreckage. Some said this just showed that international communism was at work even in Zimbabwe. Destabilising, that's the word.

All this, of course, confused people considerably. Anne and I did our job of observing and I wrote about all this to Walter Martin. In his reply he said that he had passed my letter to the Foreign Office. I was a little sorry about this, as it might make me unpopular with Soames and his staff.

And it did. No invitations to the government garden party, let alone to dinner. Our daughter, out for the Christmas vacation, was at the same college as the Soames' son – but she didn't get any invitation either.

Afterwards I was very glad. The rulers need to know what is being said, even if it's untrue, even if it's unpleasant.

Well, the election came and went and of course Mugabe won by a landslide of votes. Then the really unpleasant things began to happen. Once he had consolidated his position, the Shona Mugabe set out to cope with an internal opposition, not the white farmers yet, but the other tribe, the Ndebele. He unleashed his formidable Korea-experienced 5th Brigade to torture and massacre 15,000 of the harmless people in the south of the country. They must have regretted its independence.

Sri Lanka

The chief minister rattled through the formal pretensions of servile gratitude for not having them all shot – or it felt like that – ending sub-vocally 'and loyal farts to the Double Dutch for selling us to the bloody Brits'. Then they all got down to the business of the day which, as usual, was extremely difficult.

The trouble was that Sri Lanka, previously Ceylon, was a really difficult place. A large area of the north of the country was populated by Hindus rather than the national majority of Buddhists. It seems shocking that religions groupings dislike each other much more than do most groups comparable in other respects. The difference in this case was aggravated because the northern Hindus were mostly better educated and therefore had more prestigious and better-paid jobs than the majority of Buddhists. The problem for the government was to deal with this imbalance without offending either group too much (a certain amount was inevitable).

There were sinister rumours of a large-scale Tamil offensive against the Singhalese. Nobody knew, however, who was involved or the location of their base, if they had one. I met some people in Geneva who had ideas, but these were very vague. Eventually, however, it became clear that there was probably a militant Tamil group based on Madras (which is the capital of the Indian state of Tamil Nadu). One of my colleagues was a Tamil who grew up not in India but in Burma.

So we went to Madras, talked to people (at least he did), and listened. After a couple of days two men came round after dark, rather tentatively. In the following days we met these militant Tamils. There were four groups of rebels who all hated each other more than they collectively hated the government on which the Tamils were to wage war for more than twenty brutal, blood-filled years. Indeed we had hardly left the bickering recruits before they were at each other's throats. Of the four groups only one, the Tigers, survived the internecine blood bath, and so became immensely powerful. In fact, in a quite bizarre interlude, an Indian force of 50,000 men invaded Sri Lanka, supposedly to support the Tamils who for some reason turned against it and drove it out with a force of less than 10,000. During this bizarre interlude the president, Premadasa, fixed up a temporary truce with the Tamil Tigers, arranging for some of the leaders to stay in the grandest Colombo hotel, occupying a whole floor and served by a private lift.

Strangely enough, a quite different and very serious conflict had arisen some fifteen years before, but in the 1980s was recrudescent.

Young men and a fair number of young women, all Buddhists, living in the south of the country and reasonably well-educated, felt they were even more discriminated against than the Hindu youngsters of the north. This may well be true. The various ministries were crammed with young men (mainly) waiting to waylay the officials and plead their case.

But this didn't last. The youngsters became angry and then violent. But the violence was systematic and was well-organised by a man called Wijewira, who named it Janata Vimukhti Peramuna (JVP). At first the government did the usual thing of not taking it very seriously. But eventually the then prime minister, a woman, decided that the situation was getting out of hand: it must be put down with all necessary violence. Altogether around 15,000 young people were killed and I have no available count of the official dead, but it must have been considerable. Wijewira was sentenced to eight years in prison after making an eloquent Marxist oration.

Everyone thought that was the end of the story, but in about 1985 it was rumoured that the movement was stirring again. Before long it was in full blast. The main targets of its wrath were government workers from the president (who narrowly escaped death) to humble local village workers. Two thousand were said to have been slain. They also called 'Hartals', days when no one was to go out, smoke, listen to the radio or watch TV. Defiance of these 'rules' could be punished by death. Bodies of those killed were to be hanged outside their homes. If the body were cut down and buried, the family had to rebury it at the cost of being themselves executed. Piles of smouldering bodies were piled at road sides, trees were festooned with corpses and the rivers were choked with human remains – no one felt like eating fish for many weeks.

To a certain point in their insurrection, the JVP were winning the battle. The government had somehow lost their nerve. Then the JVP made a great tactical mistake. The ordinary soldiers had some sympathy with the rebels, many of whom came from the same stratum of society. They tended to give the JVP a chance to escape. If, for example, they were caught putting up illegal JVP posters, they would shout rather than shoot.

However, the JVP over-confidently sent messages to the army that all soldiers should desert, but if they did not, the JVP would kill their families. This move was both extremely unpleasant and very foolish. The soldiers, who had carried out their orders efficiently but without great zeal, were outraged, and terrified for their families. They hunted and killed the JVP remorselessly.

Premadasa was horrified by the slaughter and consulted my brilliant colleague John, who was based in Colombo, whereas I was back and forth from England. He even called me personally in the hopes that the earlier generation of JVP could help to find and warn him and the present activists to escape. The cynic will be sure that this was a crafty ruse. But it was not. He swore that he wanted to make peace, to save lives. His roots were twined with those of the soldiers (not the posh Sandhurst-trained officers!).

I did not, while in England, manage to get any information of use to the president, but a mysterious message was delivered to me. It said there would be an attempt on his life in three days, but that if I were with him throughout the day it would deter the assassin; he must also remain in his personal office area. I realised that might all be complete nonsense, but did not feel I could take the risk that it was not. If I took a flight on the next day, I could arrive in time.

When I reached my hotel in Colombo, I called the president. He took what I had to tell him calmly but seriously and said he would send a car to pick me up early the next morning.

The president was relaxed and cheerful, but I was relieved that he thought the warning serious. John came to lunch, but afterwards Premadasa said that, despite the warning, he must go to a meeting at the secretariat. I said that if he must he must, but that the driver should be instructed to take an unusual route.

As we set out the president said he had been told that this car was bullet-proof. 'Perhaps,' he said, 'we shall have a chance to find out.' But we didn't. It was after dark when we left the secretariat and arrived back at his compound (his office area, living quarters, temple and museum were in a compound in the Colombo slum where he was born). As I got out of the car, I felt sure that any danger there might have been was now past. Premadasa said he felt the same.

I must go back a few weeks. John had been trying to develop a contact with the

JVP. Eventually he contacted a young man called Guyian, who brought two or three other young men and women. The JVP system of security was very tight; they operated out of cells consisting of only a few individuals, receiving instructions from someone of the next rank of cells, who presumably passed them on the same way. John's young people never mentioned JVP. Guyian, however, was obviously part of the network. He would give us messages that could only come from the JVP leadership. We would take them to Premadasa who would express views that we could pass to Guyian.

There was a convergence of views which was both exciting and satisfying. Premadasa said, 'I know that if they would come to Colombo we could very easily sort everything out. I accept what they say. Just bring them here.' And he also kept repeating, 'But there's very little time.'

His position was strange. He was the president. The army was under his control, and he could not check them doing their proper job. However, he dreaded the slaughter and devastation that their success would mean. And possibly he dreaded even more the lost possibility of building a more egalitarian society – one living up to the ideals of the JVP!

But if we found Wijiwira, how would we bring him back? The army would never let us take 'their' prize. We would be shot instantly. 'Oh, dear,' the generals would say. 'How unfortunate, these good people just ran into the line of fire, too bad. But the main thing is, we have got the villains.'

But we devised a plan which we thought would foil the military. It was that we would go with a large protective convoy of vehicles from a number of embassies to meet Wijiwira and a few of the top JVP leaders, and so with them to the president in Colombo. At this stage I personally left, feeling optimistic, for a long-arranged assignment in Australia.

But the plan was never put to the test: the army got there first. They found their prey living like a country gentleman on his tea estate with his wife and five children. He was immediately carted off to Colombo (probably with his second-in-command and one or two others). I don't know exactly what happened, but it seems that the army was determined to act conclusively and without discussion. It was rumoured that the leaders were immediately tortured, and killed. The JVP structure was shattered and thousands of young people were unceremoniously slaughtered. We never found out what had happened to our brave young friends, except for Guyian who has somehow been identified; it was but slight relief to discover that this had not occurred through his association with us.

I never retuned to Sri Lanka after leaving (and expecting to come back) for Australia. Understandably, John was particularly grieved. He wrote letters to a number of people about the situation, telling the president he had done so. He never got an answer. One day, Christmas day in fact, while he and his family were at a church service, what looked like a murder squad were seen outside John's home, and were apparently frightened away by a friend who had come to visit .

John telephoned, much more casually than I would have done, and we urged him to fly back to England as soon as possible. He did so, and the international diplomatic community did brilliantly what we had hoped they might have been able to do for the JVP leaders.

Premadasa was killed about three years later. A young man on a bicycle rode up to the president who was attending a Buddhist ceremony and detonated an explosive-filled garment, killing the president and twenty-three other people

That was the end of this part of the story.

(PS. A few years later the 'wicked' JVP was jointly in charge of the government.)

Osijek

Early in 1992 Anne and I attended a large meeting on peace and development in Europe. It was held in Bratislava, now the capital of Slovakia. After my experiences in Africa, I was very interested in the relationship of these two topics, which I believed to be intricately linked, and attended meetings on the subject. There was considerable interest in it, particularly in training for work in the field. As a result I met a most active and intelligent young woman, Vesna, from Croatia, who invited me to a conference to be held in Osijek in June. I was delighted to accept.

At this time the latest round of the Balkan wars, which triggered the First World War, was being waged ferociously. The Serbs had begun the conflict by attacking Slovenia in the previous year, but had withdrawn for several reasons, primarily because the distance between Serbia and Slovenia would make for logistical errors, and anyway an unfriendly Croat population lay between.

Instead the sizeable Serb population was encouraged to rise against the Croats in and around Osijek. But before long this 'unofficial' war became a real, international conflict in which Croatia lost nearly a third of its area to jubilant Serbia. Osijek was not over-run, but it was occupied on three sides, and lost eleven hundred dead and ten times that many injured. Despite these losses the population had swollen with refugees from the areas occupied by Serbia.

Strong pressure from the UN brought the brutal bombardment of Osijek to an end at about the time that the conference was held, although parts of the town were still considered dangerous to walk in.

The conference took place as planned. A small international group came up by train from Zagreb, a five hour zig-zag journey to avoid the Serb-occupied territory. Our immediate impression of Osijek was pathetically symbolic of hopeful progress thwarted by brutal reality: the town's new post office – shattered. It was fine, it was beautifully designed, but had been made of glass.

The conference turned out not to be very successful. It was fairly well attended by people who were not very interested. Some indeed were hostile. They were not interested in peace; they wanted to get on with giving the Serbs a bloody nose, though how was not clear, since Osijek was in a state of semi-siege – there were even said to be crafty Serb snipers within the city. But the great plus for me was getting to know some of the people who were to become my dearest friends. I cou[ld] mention many names but will just refer to Katarina Kruhonja, who with Kru[no] were the joint founders of the peace movement – not that it was yet a movemen[t] but a joint revulsion against war. Katarina was Catholic and a physician wh[o] specialised in nuclear medicine, and Kruno an atheist and philosophical soci[al] scientist, a powerful pair.

Katarina and I became deep friends, and still are. We had the opportunity [to] become very close. I stayed in her apartment in one of the tower blocks so prev[a]lently constructed during the communist period of Eastern Europe – her apartme[nt] had sustained two direct hits when the shelling was most intense and her labor[a]tory was also hit, scattering nuclear waste far and wide. We got to know each oth[er] very well in the early mornings doing last night's washing up. This cemented o[ur] friendship and my admiration for Katarina's high intelligence and spirited dete[r]mination to work for peace in spite of the general hostility of many leading citizen[s]. Particular among these was the warlord who had defended Osijek brilliantly b[ut] ruthlessly.

The conference only lasted two days, but I felt at the end that the green sho[ot] of peace could grow if given time and space. I thought that if a smaller group cou[ld] meet together for a longer time, they might be able to develop a practical plan [of] activities to help the bereaved or injured and other victims of the war. I then t[old] Katarina that if she agreed to this, I would be glad to come over for some days [to] go more deeply into the problems of peace if she could arrange for a group of fifte[en] to twenty people really concerned about peace to meet together.

In two weeks the meeting took place. It lasted five days, with a slightly shifti[ng] membership of about twenty attending. About half way through something ve[ry] significant took place. Up until that time, everyone spoke for themselves – 'I thi[nk] I agree, I don't agree, I like.' After that everything changed. 'We think, we agre[e].' Another said, 'I'll take the minutes,' 'send them out,' 'organise the coffee,' and [so] on. We were suddenly transformed from a collection of individuals to a grou[p of] people of a like mind.

And so, miraculously, it has remained for a dozen years. Katarina visited [me] here in England a few weeks ago. She's the same, but the work she began j[ust] before we met has expanded into almost every dimension of national life and mu[ch] wider. She and Vesna, who suggested I visited Osijek, were together awarded [the] Alternate Nobel Prize (as the Right Livelihood Award is known). It is presente[d in] the same manner as the regular Nobel, but the day before and in the same par[t of] the Swedish parliament, and the supper afterwards is marvellous.

But it wasn't always like that.

One day when I was not with them, Katarina and Kruno went to see the m[an] who was in effect deputy warlord.

When Katarina asked some not very crucial question, he burst into a tirad[e.] How could she be so impudent? Did she not realise she owed her life to clemency? The town was full of people who so resented her unpatriotic indifference to the sufferings of others. They bitterly resented her wanting to make peace with the bestial Serbs who had slaughtered their husband, son, father and so on. There was a group of women he actually had to stop planning to lynch her and he couldn't always restrain them. And the soldiers too. They said their fingers itched on the trigger if they saw Katarina and Kruno. He wouldn't prosecute anyone whose patience wore out.

Katarina and Kruna went to the door. She turned round and said, 'Perhaps we can have another talk before too long.'

The warlord looked abashed and muttered something noncommittal.

That evening several of us had a long and somewhat worried discussion. Was there anything we could do to improve the safety of Katarina and others without surrendering any of our principles? We thought of a few, such as discussing the issue with some of the clergy, but nothing particularly significant.

The next day I had to go back to England for a couple of weeks, and was very anxious about what I might find on my return. I was delighted to find, however, that all my friends seemed to be happy and carefree instead of grimly determined. But they were neither. When I asked them how they could be so light-hearted when under such menace, they said, 'When our minds were irrevocably made up, well, we all felt liberated.' And so did I.

I think it was about this time when the spirit of the peace centre, and the courageous initiative of its members, began to be appreciated by and to spread into the wider community.

Indications of general acceptance encouraged Katarina to invite local residents and people from the neighbouring villages to come with their children for a day of music and dancing, games, fun, exhibitions of art, and of general good fellowship. I thought it was a splendid idea, but our (then) very modest centre was in a corner of the crumbling cloister of an ancient vacated monastery in the picturesque old part of the city – and was next door to the military headquarters. Since the army had the reputation for disliking the peace supporters, I was afraid they might sabotage the party and maybe beat up the peace supporters. But not a bit of it. They joined in some of the fun and actually contributed to the cost of the lunch.

Thereafter the work of the centre spread wisely throughout the city and later into the whole region of East Slovenia. It did so on two main fronts. Firstly, as indeed from its inception, the centre concentrated on practical work to help people who had suffered through the war – through bereavement or injury, loss of home through shelling, loss of job through displacement, interrupted education, separation of families. The suspicious warlords classified these activities as 'charitable', but considered them to be a crafty trick to allay suspicions and then spread subversive talk of peace.

It was indeed true that the influence of the centre did spread, seeping into the consciousness of the people of Osijek, not seditiously, however, but helpfully and constructively. Moreover, this work was done in a spirit of personal concern ar caring, very far from the impersonal conscientious approach of officialdom.

This I believe to be, in the full sense the words, work for peace. Its underlyir effect seemed to be decontaminating minds of their illusions, anger and confusio Other peace work in which I have been involved may have been apparent successful in achieving the objective of some ruler or political party. All too ofte these objectives have not coincided with the sensible hopes of the majority of t people.

In other places some of the official local authorities have made angry noisc 'The treacherous do-gooders (a dangerous crew!) have persisted in their campaig of disloyalty.' But, says the official mind, it's hard to catch them out, they are ve clever. You won't find them doing anything exactly illegal, and in fact they we publicly praised for their feeding programmes and ambulance work in the bat zone. Moreover, when the war came to an end, people forgot that it was we wh had stopped them from being massacred.

Fortunately Katarina and her friends did not have quite such a displeasir opposition to cope with. They did not seem to be affected, or only to a very sm; extent, by the Black Cloud syndrome. They were far too busy! In fact on mo recent visits I have been struck by the mental clarity of the people I met.

It is important to stress, however, that Katarina and the peace centre are n important for what they have done, but for developing a way of organisation a practice that is crucially important as a form of peace-making. I said earlier th war, including highly victorious war, could not be fought without loss. T campaigns of the Osijek peace centre, however, are not fought with weapor except courage and goodwill, and with no objective, except the well-being of the clients – the young, the sick, the bereaved, the hungry, the old.

These may indeed represent an obscure threat to the deranged (who are a potential clients!), but to no other enemy. They neither demand nor expect a reward – this may be annoying! By the same token they may, having no speci political party policy except to expedite the well-being of the needy, actually ser a multitude of urgent needs – or indeed argue forcefully with those they consid ill-advised or mischievous. This role is somewhat similar to that of the Red Cro but conceivably with a more open role.

Finally, it is important to mention the inherent (as I believe) but unspecifi spiritual essence of the centre's work and general part in society. There is room believers in more than one creed or, of course, none. The 'faith' of the centre a body is indeterminate.

It is perhaps worth attempting to elaborate the centre's approach to ideology. I carry my own views with me and can refer mainly back to material Part 1 of this book. I think that the ideal state of mind is emptiness. That is to s that our Mind (which is an offshoot of the Mind of the Universe) is, genera speaking, muddled and confused (I use the word 'cluttered'). Thus we may fail understand, or to take advantage of, the wider world of the Universe for both service to be carried out and wisdom to be gained. In general, our rather muddled creeds or ideologies create difficulties for us in reaching a clear-cut understanding of ourselves and the world. This is intensified by what I have referred to as the Black Cloud, an emanation of the despair, pain and confusion after nearly a century of terrible bloodshed and human cruelty.

But talk of creeds and ideologies, of what you or I believe, slides very close to Self – which blocks our openness to the Mind of the Universe, bringing us down to a limited personal level.

We must struggle to redeem this surrender.

Global relations

Humans and the cosmos

Previous chapters aimed to give a high priority to the position of us humans in the cosmos, despite our frequent failures. In this chapter we will consider more particular aspects of our existence. And I use the word 'failure', thinking of myself and others, let alone the collective hash we have made of our world. Why not we, the majority, who have created such horrors? That is what we shall be discussing in this and following pages – I hope.

It is by no means absurd to suggest that many people have achieved the impossible psychologically. I have in mind the victims of great cruelty, whose power of love and reconciliation has wrought miracles (however one interprets the word). Understanding this, we feel free. We recognise that we only actually know through our connection with others. This is the reason why solitary confinement is so shattering: the essential web of interconnection has been largely broken. Equally, of course, it is terrible for any of us to be he herded interminably together.

The subtleties and complexities of the Universe are obviously not to be plumbed by using larger and more sophisticated telescopes or more searching analyses of the soil chemistry of stars, but basically in our own minds. Here we need hard work to clear the obstruction of imperfect thinking. We need meditation exercises to free us from the prison of irrational thought.

To the extent that we come to terms with these facts, we feel free, liberated from an archaic shibboleth.

I have not known how to treat the topic of angels. These beings are known and respected all over the world. They are kindly, they go around helping people, some of them serve in many cultures as guardian angels who take special care of individuals. They are in an entirely different league from gnomes, fairies, hobbits and others who are mostly terrestrial and not much given to good works except the fairies, and those are largely fictional. But the angels are widely liked and respected. But where do they come from? They seem to live on the wing except when helping their clients.

My own opinion, which is not to be trusted, is that they may be elements of those advanced human beings who (or I should perhaps say 'which') have been marked out (but by whom?) to serve as angels. If there are indeed such beings, unless they are part of a worldwide illusion, this would seem as reasonable an explanation as any.

I say with all humility that one of my uncles seems to have been fine angel material. He was drowned in his late thirties, when his ship was sunk in the battle of Jutland. He made a profound impression on many people, for many reasons. He was extremely good looking (photographs show this to be true): he was a fine scholar and a Fellow (they actually call them Students) of his Oxford college, Christ Church. He was a superb cricketer. He was deeply loved by many, and although he nearly married more than once, he told my mother (who loved him dearly) that something always held him back. When he died, the Poet Laureate, Robert Bridges, wrote a poem in his memory which was published in *The Times* among many other tributes.

My mother, like many other bereaved women, went to a well-known medium, Mrs Merrill I think was her name, who called him back.

He told my mother through the medium that he had only returned to reassure her that there was 'life after death', but asked her firmly not to contact him again, as he was busily engaged with other important work.

Globalization

I was delighted when the word 'globalization' appeared on the world's mental screen. I thought that all the people I had encountered in the poor areas of the world would now be getting the help they needed to clamber out of the deep ditches of poverty with their slippery sidewalks.

I knew so many who were strong, intelligent, or devoted to some cause or person, but were held back by poverty, by living in a poor, disorganized nation, by lack of hospitals or adequate schools, or sometimes by corrupt or treacherous officials.

Now, surely, with the magnificent means of rapid communication by plane and radio, the energetic, skilful and good-hearted representatives of modern business, charities and benign international agencies, they should be out of the woods (or deserts and jungles).

But of course, as I and almost everyone else now knows, it didn't work out exactly like this. Big business, a term which of course covers a multitude of activities, saw and naturally exploited an infinity of opportunities for profit (and profit means power which means yet more profit). The international agencies, mainly the World Bank and the International Monetary Fund, were (and are) largely controlled by Americans, who although genuinely doing their best for their 'clients', have values which are American rather than African, Asian, etc. These, of course, are often inappropriate. Big business is most notorious for its money-grubbing pharmaceutical policies, which are more profitable to the shareholders than to victims of malaria or AIDS.

Well, after all, business is business!

But the charitable organizations are beyond praise – the Red Cross and Red Crescent, Oxfam, Save the Children, MSF rightly so well-known that its initials suffice. And even the IMF deserves an occasional faint cheer.

Globalization, however, does not. It has proved the flop of the century – except, of course, for the Big Eight.

At this point I hear a faint protest from the World Trade Organization (sometimes referred to as the World Trip Off). It may be remembered that in the late summer of 2004, an agreement was reached by all parties, the relatively much more numerous poorer countries and the relatively much smaller group of the rich ones. This was hailed as a triumph of egalitarian democracy. In fact the poorer nations, after a prolonged and difficult argument, decided that they would lose what minor concessions they had won if they annoyed the rich by pressing for any further leniency.

My main purpose, however, is not so much to describe and criticize institutions, but Mind and its condition. These, however, are largely inseparable. Globalization and its various organizational structures clearly have a considerable effect on how millions of people think and feel (and they all do so differently). Some are angry, some avaricious, some hopeful, some disappointed, and so on. But there are certain collective feelings derived from the experience of a *new civilization*. Globalization imparts a whole new set of values. These are essentially concerned with power and profit. They tend to make us more dependent on money than previously and thus to develop a financial 'philosophy' of life. This, depending on circumstances, makes us affected, more or less, by external forces of the market, of the contemporary fashion, of aspects of the international scene previously not noticed. We feel that our whole identity (which has suddenly become very important) depends on a variety of conditions: things, skills, clothes, and so on. The rich want a different gratification from the poor and the poor want a quite different gratification from the rich (except perhaps to become rich themselves), but they equally all want the self-symbols of success. This basically means that everyone craves to believe that s/he is better than everyone else.

The main criticism of this system of globalization is insensate stupidity. The rich and the would-be rich, obsessed with the gratification of their desires (which they call their 'needs'), have no space in their narrowed hearts to consider that happiness comes from peace and love within. Other human beings, including such 'loved ones' as friends and children, mainly exist as means to gratify each other's egos. They have no understanding of each other, or wish to do so. The reality of human life is alien to them. They may be scholarly or technically skilled, but without any understanding of the human heart, they sorely lack the sensitivity and insight which are essential to wise and indeed to all effective action – to personal contentment. But does this not remind us of the Black Cloud? It certainly reminds me, though not with surprise. The atmosphere of strain and misery, the dense unhappiness, the heartless greed, the lack of humanity are all too familiar: the ever more enveloping mass of self-perpetuating global infirmity typified by the senseless collective distemper of our sad and violent age.

To sum up, this is what globalization has achieved. Firstly, at its most mundane level, it has created a social system which benefits the rich, and further impoverishes the poor (with a few pliable Uncle Toms over whom the wealthy slobber in fraudulent hypocrisy). Then there is a well-crafted economic system to bolster rich business-buggers, as they are generally called. These skilfully structured arrangements have succeeded in laying the foundations of an excellent two-tier civilization. In this, the upper and the lower classes inevitably hate each other, and provide endless wars in which the wealthy countries arrange fine practical training for their armies. This has the additional advantage of culling a considerable number of the second tier without any political complications.

From another standpoint, however, this situation provides a convenient cause for the second tier activists to launch what the first tier call terrorist attacks.

This lamentable situation should encourage the rest of the world's population, if there are a sufficient number, to unravel the iniquitous and chaotic imbroglio.

The principal highway to Mind

The principal highway to Mind is love. Many of us are driving along it by car. (However, there are also a number of us on the side roads, footpaths, tracks and the like which lead us to less, very much less, desirable spots.) The travellers on the highway, however, are far from necessarily in cars: they may be travelling in carts drawn by horses or even by donkeys, or on bicycles, or on foot. If they are going by car, it may not be the newest or fastest model.

It's like that with love. Those who truly love will go on the highway however much they lack those things that the world values – intelligence, money, skills, charm, good looks and other delightful attributes. There is a suggestive Tibetan legend to reveal what happened to a dim-witted man who hoped to become a monk. His teacher asked him to memorise a short devotional book, after which he could be ordained. But he failed completely. His kindly teacher then asked the young man progressively to memorise shorter and shorter passages of the book. But in the end he couldn't cope with even a single line. The teacher then gave up, saying, 'Never mind, you are a good young man. You are doing a fine job sweeping the floor; just keep it up.'

So the young man did as his teacher recommended, efficiently, devotedly and without a word of complaint.

The abbot of the monastery, however, had taken note of the young man and decided that he would not only be a fine monk, but actually the abbot of a monastery. The monks were furious. How could this idiot possibly be considered as their spiritual superior?

The angry monks decided to have their revenge on their new 'so-called' abbot. They designed the traditional throne, but too high for him to mount it. They waited sniggering for his arrival. When he came, however, he merely glanced at it and waved a hand at the throne which sank to a manageable height. But instead of mounting it, the new abbot flew into the air whence, circling around the hall, he delivered a most erudite and learned lecture for many hours.

The monks were fascinated and completely won over.

Great illusion

We are ignorant of the mind we have. We believe we want something that doesn't exist, and are unhappy when we don't get it. This makes us angry with our friends, blaming them for our unhappiness, and we continue to crave, and to rage against the people and circumstances which we blame for our disappointment for our failure to be happy. And all this further confuses our mind.

This sad cycle is as predictable as it was two-and-a-half thousand years ago in the time of the Buddha, who referred to this sorry cycle as the Three Poisons – which still infest us. We need only to scan the papers to be assured by the advertisements that we can achieve our goal of sublime happiness by purchasing that car or by going on this cruise. We don't, of course, believe it – well, not entirely, but to some extent. If we didn't, the advertising industry would collapse. But the car or holiday would (probably) give us some pleasure. And so they should, but not quiet contentment. Not, for example, the peaceful contentment of family life despite the ups and downs. The car/vacation legitimately bring a substitute for real happiness. True happiness is the sweetest fruit of love. But the essence of love is the absence of Self.

First is last

Something amazing happened over Christmas, 1914. British and German soldiers invaded each other's trenches. But they left their weapons behind. Instead they brought beer and wine and bits and pieces of sausage and mince pies and all. Best of all, they brought friendliness and good cheer.

'Bloody war,' they said, 'Well, I suppose we've got to get it over, but as quickly as possible. Maybe next Christmas we'll be able to visit each other's homes and laugh about it all and the fucking officers and all that. Have another drink, mate.'

The officers prowled around. They couldn't very well take part in the fun (some of them may even have liked to), but they also didn't want to seem stand-offish. Anyway, they didn't know if it wasn't all a bit risky – but then, Christmas was Christmas.

Well, it wasn't. When the stuffy old generals of both sides heard about it, there was hell to pay. The shit really hit the fan. A few of the men were court-martialled and condemned to be shot, to discourage this sort of fraternization. The officers were also court-martialled and reduced to the ranks. British and German senior officers were equally furious at this shocking outrage. So bad for discipline!

And the filthy war went on and on and on ...

Conclusion

I had contemplated writing a concluding section that would take our human steps beyond the period of this first decade. I would have enjoyed the speculation, but on further consideration I realised that I was neither a social nor a political analyst.

What I do know something about is what I would have called the state of the soul. People in general think of the soul as the essence or real or permanent aspect of their nature. If they believe in God, they may think of the soul as being the fragment of divinity within them which will return to its source, it is hoped unsullied, when they die. I certainly respect those who seriously and thoughtfully believe in and care for the soul, as do believing Christians and Muslims (though I fear some extremists do not).

I have come, however, to form a somewhat – I could almost say similar, but will settle for comparable – understanding. I believe that every living thing, large or small, is an entity but not an entirety. That is to say, it is something to be preserved and valued while the life force holds it together, but as death comes, or to put it accurately, dissolution, the entity breaks up. This means that the various essences continue as components of other, perhaps greater, organisms or minds, to merge unto a vaster Emptiness. Thus the goal of our existence at every level is to coalesce with ever more creative beings and to contribute with increasing significance to the life of the planet and perhaps beyond.

I trust that this explanation of my beliefs will not offend any reader, or seem incompatible with what I have written. I think that the most questionable, but equally important, of my ideas concerns the Black Cloud, whether confined to the earth or spreading upwards. I believe and have repeatedly explained that this is the projection of the pain, despair and misery of millions resulting from the suffering of war and hardship, mainly during the last hundred years. I may be mistaken, but the innumerable wars, large-scale social disturbances, injustices, domination by the wealthy and great increases in mental illness are surely clear indications of a sick society, which means a damaged and generally unhappy population.

I wrote a book on this theme, *To Tame the Hydra*, several years ago and have had no reason to change my analysis, which was rather more social-psychological than philosophical (as these pages modestly are). It seemed to me that the combination of globalization (not only in the economic sense) was stimulating desires based on the enormous opportunities which were currently available. These, however, were withheld, or appeared to be, by the greed of those who already enjoyed them.

There is nothing new in this except its virtual universality and a subtle shift in our perception of happiness. This is the belief now very widely shared that happiness is based on things that are external to us. I had a most enlightening experience (described in *To Tame the Hydra*). When I was five, I learned that a new toy did not bring lasting joy. That came only from within.

I have been attacked since then for belonging to the comfortable middle classes who assuage their guilt by trying to persuade the poor and suffering that all they need to do is to pray or think beautiful thoughts or to do the equivalent of contributing to Oxfam. This, however, is as much of a cop-out for those critics as their criticism of me. Any serious reflection will reveal how much happiness is autonomous, and how much fear and anxiety come from inner rather than external turmoil.

The danger which now threatens the world is that globalization (with all the hope and fear, anger and despair it generates) will disable the very strong and active movements of justice, peace and equality. Sadly, these are hated almost as much by the strongholds of most of the wealthiest governmental establishments, as are the revolutionaries such as Al Qa'ida. The latter have the support of a powerful although distorted faith, as do the zombies of the Pentagon, the White House and a few in 10 Downing Street.

So what are the odds? Who do we want to win?

Can the spirit break through the Black Cloud to let the light of reality shine on this dark scene? Will we see again, as I once did, the great shining star leading us towards truth?

Postscript

The few pages of this postscript constitute a sort of apology for the book. On re-reading *Varieties of Mind* I felt that its (that is, my) criticisms were justified. I felt, however, that some of the discussion, especially the mystical/spiritual passages in the first part, were controversial: but so they should be, unless we are slaves to a dogma which by definition cannot be argued against. Nevertheless, I could see the book as a whole would not encourage optimism, and perhaps I should have done more to support pessimism.

I must make it clear, by the way, that the controversy I have hinted at has hitherto taken place entirely within my head.

Moving outside it, I present a very simple case. Firstly, the current troubles (there are several interlocking crises) have been built up over the decades by the stupidity, greed, malignity, selfish ambition, incompetence, of armies of rulers and their similar but usually more intelligent toadies-in-office, who knew how to keep the peasants, coolies, slaves and the lower middle classes in a state of miserable and insecure dependency.

But the scene has changed somewhat. We have had our ration of slaughter for the next few decades. Now possibly the propitious moment has really come: exit the aristocracy, enter the bourgeoisie. Or whatever one likes to call it; I prefer to think of it as people who have a measure of choice in their lives and who experiment with life (to some extent) and allow themselves to act on feeling rather than necessity, to abandon the safe path for the uncertainties of a better one.

But I should stop at this point, lest I become guilty of the very confusion I hope to prevent. I have hitherto concentrated on what human beings have decided to do or to make, both in terms of how we relate to each other, or what we create, whether boiling an egg or building a house.

I also began to understand, however, that many people were, like me, unaware of the range of their minds. At the same time it became increasingly clear to me that many were not aware of their capacities. This was a long period of exploration and discovery. It began, oddly enough, when I was working with a class of post-graduates at Harvard University. One might have thought that their minds were all wide open. But they were not: their highly disciplined intelligence was in fact a handicap. But once this was broken down, the floodgates opened wide to every sort of practice and idea. The narrow precision of their types of scholarship had confined them to an intense but limited intellectual concentration which had precluded many equally important aspects of life, much of which would have been – and in fact became – a rich and fertile life from which they found many alternatives to choose.

Those students were indeed exceptional; many other people I have known were not so naturally talented. I now know, however, that there is a vast reservoir of unrecognized and therefore undeveloped mental talent latent in humanity and waiting to be realized and released. This would be an enormous boon for humanity.

I find myself now reconsidering what I had written earlier on Mind. It returns to me now with renewed force and conviction. I realize how often we have had the privileged opportunity to rediscover the wealth and universality of Mind, and sadly failed to do so.

I really did not anticipate the rapidity and sudden power of this recognition, nor the related certainty that our main job is to help others and ourselves to recognize the strength of the Mind of which we are all a part and which we must never waste.

So I think it's essential for us to change gear; instead of theorizing, to teach ourselves and each other. It is essential first of all that we understand in an *active sense*. I mean that in *practice*, not just pleasant theory, our Mind is also the offshoot of the infinitely larger Mind of the Universe (mistakenly thought of, as I believe, by many Christians as an element of the divine).

This mind of ours, though I spelt it just now with a capital M, is also human. It is also subject to human disorders some of which are due to physical flaws or infections, but also more specifically *mental* and the probable result of the clutter and confusion to which there is frequent reference in the book. Another source of mental disorder is what I call the Black Cloud. I have written a lot about this, but let me ask you to read a few more words about it. I have said that the Black Cloud is the miserable mood of fear, unhappiness, confusion that is generated by such long periods of war, oppression and misery that it is very hard to shift, either from individuals or communities. The pages on Globalization may give additional insight into this unpleasant condition.

It should, however, be treated with cheerful (though sympathetic) optimism. This is the best treatment if it is accompanied by explanation. No one likes to feel ill without being told why and the essential character of the Black Cloud is its unreality. Given the truth, it will *melt away*, but perhaps slowly.

I come to feel, therefore, that a considerable proportion of humanity has been sleeping the dreams of its confused and cluttered mind. It became indeed difficult for the great Mind of the Universe to break through the mists of incomprehension and to activate the stagnant human mind. But now it is awakening.

Among many other things, the human mind is waking up to the Black Cloud, having passively accepted its stifling dominance for many years.

Moreover, now that the human mind is becoming more alert to the Black Cloud, so is it awakening to the threat of the Selves resuming their ancient authority. This is also true: strong Selves would impede the development of the

Emptiness which accompanies the Universal Mind. Moreover there is now a larger arena where the two contestants, the Self (or ego) and the Black Cloud (the mind), will be less able to check the advance of the Universal Mind.

So what positive steps can be suggested? I suggest we start with yet another of the innumerable analyses of the contemporary scene in the Sunday papers. The general suggestion for a serious overview is naturally commonplace – but the theme is not. People in general know little about the subject of mind (except for court cases in which psychiatrists give evidence), but a skilful practitioner should be able to stir interest in the Black Cloud. I doubt, however, if the most eloquent lawyer could sell the idea of the Universal Mind. But the drama of the relationship between these celestial bodies and the depression or panic attacks suffered by ordinary people might stir the dregs of gloomy inertia into activating some degree of awareness.

Obviously there is nothing *we* can do to activate the Mind of the Universe. What is necessary is the lively zeal of our planetary members; not only for the clarification of their own minds (which we must all develop), but the hope which has largely died out in many as a result of the sickness of the Black Cloud. We must, however, strive to revive it, and with it the energy to induce change. This argument places the ball directly in our court. It is very much up to us whether or not to believe in the sort of future for which we claim to be working, whether to *believe* in its *real feasibility* – we must have done so in some measure, otherwise none of this would have been thought and written about by many people. *To do* is what is proposed here, and more; we must act, and our actions must in some measure express the sincerity of our feelings. Our professed generosity and compassion would be a blasphemous farce if our behaviour were mean and selfish. The proof of the pudding of liberality is the size of the portion shared with needy others.

But what, you may ask, do you propose that we actually *do*? Well, I feel that the philosophical/psychological ideas contained mainly in the first of the four main sections of this book, especially the ideas on Emptiness, would be more or less acceptable to most members of the faiths with the largest memberships.

I would feel it very important that members, those interested (I would not wish to prescribe the possible group at all precisely), should be the type of human being aware of human identity but aware also of links beyond our planet leading inevitably, I believe, to reciprocal enrichment.

At the moment we are, in a sense, under siege. Great and continuing damage has been done through our own folly and aberration, especially in the last hundred years, by violence and selfish greed. We both, people and planet, are implicated. The great globe is in deep distress, while enormous numbers of its people are in the grips of a psycho/physical sickness which both alienates us from the Universal Mind, and at the same time makes us yearn for its enveloping comfort.

But in this extremity, in the fearful plight of *all* life, there is growing recognition by many wise and humane, generous and thoughtful women and men, that we must *act*.

Many sorts of action will undoubtedly emerge and have indeed already done so. One is suggested in the following paragraphs.

To start with, the groups of all types, united by the same concerns, come together to discuss them, to awaken and enlarge their concerns, and to develop whatever they feel to be practical projects, psychological or technical; but always moving towards the larger and fundamentally creative Universal Mind (however they think of it and name it). There is little point in making any effort which is not in tune with the nature of the Mind. But what is it?

Is there really such a thing? I began this book with an Introduction saying that it would not be a religious work, but on later pages talked of a Universal Mind of which there is no proof, but which, in my account, seems to be what others have called the Mind of God (and no proof of that either). You may feel I am inferring that there is no such thing as God, but that there is a force which behaves like the force of God if indeed he exists.

Well, I agree and can only answer by trying to explain my own experience. Firstly, there are the separate arguments as widely apart as those of the Dalai Lama (and other Buddhists) and Richard Dawkins. On the other hand, I am impressed by the Dalai Lama's plausible statement that there must have been something to set up the whole vast system and keep it going. But I have heard Dawkins' demolishing response.

Then, however, another sort of argument began to emerge. At times when I was uncertain how, or if, to proceed, or tired and feeling in need of a break, or confused, I became aware of a gentle, friendly pressure. It was as though a loving force was insistently pushing its way through the flimsy 'protection' of the 'self' and/or the tiredness. And as this was being done, I felt, with a growing joy and wonder, so encouraged, so much less tired, truly energetic. I felt some(thing, one) actually working on me, rather like a competent, kindly masseur, who stayed with me until I was cured, then quietly retired and left me profoundly refreshed. Above all, in addition to this healing touch, this controlling presence left me *wiser*. I knew things I had not known before.

But I will also express this aspect of Being differently. It's not exactly a matter of the Outer Mind entering the Inner, but the Inner revealing itself; this self-manifestation, I then realised, was simply already a part of me, a human being, my being, now in fact coming into its magnificent inheritance. This is the reality that is dawning in me, at this moment as I touch the keys. It represents another level of reality, the Unity of the All – from the nerves that direct these fingers on the keyboard, to the majestic Absolute.

Let us understand and rejoice.

Notes on inter-species permeability

These Notes make no claim to present new facts or theories. On the contrary, they suggest how, within the compass of a small family, they raise perennial questions regarding the relationship of humans and animals – the latter including, in this case, even Lepidoptera. More generally, however, the main issues are ones of porosity: in what respects do we impinge on each other's behaviour, thoughts and feelings? This question of course has many implications on both sides, especially if the animals are pets or creatures that we eat.

It is most satisfactory that the amateurish curiosity of many past decades has now evolved into the respected field of ethology. Indeed one university colleague of mine, Niko Tinbergen, won the Nobel Prize for work in this field, and was recognised, with Konrad Lorenz, as legitimizing the discipline. In addition, another colleague, John Bowlby, a child psychiatrist, was linked in related research, thus widening the field of interconnected life studies.

I would like to be able to think, finally, that what I have tentatively referred to as Cosmic Anthropology may be carried forward as energetically and wisely as those I have just mentioned did their own fields. I am, however, not simply concerned for the promotion of scholarly endeavour, but for the wiser understanding of life so desperately needed by our planet.

My mother was known to young and old as Cork and thus (as she would have preferred) I shall refer to her here. Among her friends were some most unlikely intimates, old women met casually on the top of a bus, for example, while her closest friend was a French woman who lived in the slums of Boulogne. But her most startling relationships were with non-humans.

Some of these relationships involved a reciprocal amity and sympathy, not just slavish adoration, as between devoted dog and master, though even in most extreme emotional subjugation there will probably be some reciprocity. I shall shortly give some examples, but will stress now more straightforward instances of affinity.

While we were on holiday in France, Cork persuaded a villager to sell her a nest of baby birds which he had intended to bake in a pie for his children. She brought them back to England, feeding them with the end of a pipette. The baby birds eventually learned to fly and they fluttered around nearby. However, they all eventually fell victims to various predators – cats and hawks, most probably.

But the first day of springtime when we were back in the room that we had used the previous summer, in flew the last of the little birds. It circled Cork chirping – and dropped dead. Cork told us that she had had a comparable experience as a girl. A peacock butterfly she had known the previous summer had reappeared, flown around her, and died.

The most telling example of permeability was the badger, Wadge as Cork named her. She, like the little birds, came from a farmer's wife who knew of Cork's ability with young creatures. Wadge had to be fed with a pipette – indeed the one used for the chicks. She spent most of the time lying on Cork's lap and, when not feeding or sleeping, she played with the buttons on her dress.

As she developed, however, she acquired strange habits. One was unpacking. The family had moved to the country from London with many crates and boxes holding different types of china and kitchen ware – different sized plates, dishes, tureens, cups and so on. Others contained various types of glass. To start with Cork, hearing worrying movements upstairs, would go to investigate. Wadge would come to the door irritably, Cork was sure, as if to say, 'I'm very busy, please don't interrupt'. The business that she was engaged with was unpacking plates and dishes from the crates and stacking them by type on the floor: big plates with other big plates, small with small, tureens with tureens and so on. This task took all her concentration and our presence was thoroughly distracting.

Wadge and Julius (always known as Juli), my puppy bought for two shillings and six pence from the local farm, were good friends. They particularly enjoyed pranks in which Wadge was always the leader. Two of these were sabotaging the living room: they tore the curtains and the frills on sofas. The next was more ambitious: they not only tore things up, but upset flower pots and actually went to the lengths of biting off dead flowers from the beds outside to spread around the living room. As a delicate last touch they broke open a box of skin ointment and smeared the contents all over the place.

What strikes me as the most brilliant and ingenious of their caprices was the Attack on the Picnic Table. Several of the humans (mostly adult) were enjoying a tea set out on a table in a little grove of busy trees. We were aware from previous experience that Juli and/or Wadge were table raiders and on this occasion were determined to protect a particularly fine uncut cake.

We had a good view in front and when, before long, we saws Juli dashing towards us and then trying to leap on the table, we were prepared to repel his advance and did so successfully.

Meanwhile, however, Wadge had crept towards us through the shrubbery. While we were dealing with Juli, she had jumped on the table, seized the cake and hurried to a (presumably) prearranged rendezvous with Juli.

We soon found them there, eating the cake.

Finally, I should mention two affairs in which Juli alone was implicated.

Juli reacted strongly to music. He howled when Cork played the piano, and indeed much later when I played the flute. While Cork and I were away, Cork's sister, Adeline, and her husband Ralph Vaughan Williams, the composer, were living in the house. Ralph spent much of his time using the piano as an aid to composition; we have a photo of Juli with his head on Ralph's knee and his lips shaped consistently with soft singing. I just wish we had a recording to check with the howl that I remember.

I had the good fortune to watch the second Juli incident.

I entered the room where the breakfast had been laid, to see Juli on his back legs, head craning across the table with jaws open and about to close on a bun.

I started at him, astonished at this act of defiant temerity. Juli looked back at me with an expression (I thought) of frozen horror. However, he quickly seemed to have realised that, having been flagrantly caught in the act, there was no point in pretending he had done nothing wrong. Instead, he decided to turn it into a joke.

He took hold of the bun in his mouth, pranced around a little, then tossed it in the air a couple of times and caught it. Then he wagged his tail (affably – that was my human interpretation) – as much as to say, 'Oh, I'm just having a bit of fun, fun with a bun'.

Abbreviated version for readers in a hurry

To disarm the mind

To disarm the mind,
the All, the everything, the sea in which
the galaxies and time interminable swim
through sweeping currents of the universe,
the essence of all things that be
and have been and will ever be –
Mind, the powerhouse of emptiness,
the Void.

Looking through the microscope at planet earth,
almost imperceptible in its
tiny solar system across the Milky Way,
it appears to be infected.
Superficially, it seems
it won't explode
or swerve off track, or anything dramatic
but the miniscule corpuscles we call life
could gradually disappear.
No cosmic harm in that, of course,
just the conclusion of a rather
interesting enterprise.

More detailed investigation seems to show
one type of life, a germ called homo,
has generated gases and various
toxic substances that damage the
environment within which they live,
a fact which might suggest
their limited intelligence,
or we should say, ones in whom

perfection is obscured by
clouds of ignorant illusion.

But beyond this folly, for reasons which
are almost incomprehensible,
they are addicted to destroying
not just their precious biosphere,
but each other.

To this end they have devised
machines which specialise in slaughter.
Some indeed can wipe out many thousands
in a single blast.

One might well think the suicidal murder
(for all must suffer equally)
of these poor maddened creatures
would not be much regretted,
but we are one,
the galaxies, the planets and the stars,
the entire mighty cosmos we inhabit,
the endless void,
even poor homo wiping itself out
in grievous suffering
upon its tiny star,
even this minute
inconsequential species,
just as are the stars and satellites,
is part of our great Whole,
a fragment of perfection.

Nothing is separate,
our loneliness is an illusion.
We share the pains and the confusions, the joys and peaceful days
of all our many, very varied selves;
the totality is sacred.

The lens now focused on the planet earth
reveals the intricacies of the world
homunculus has wrought.

It concentrates on two phenomena,

manifested separately, but knit together.

The first is multiple examples of
the operation of the Profit Motive.
This implies that they believe there's virtue in
acquiring, by whatever ruse they can,
the wealth and power that would free them
from restraints of care and charity.
It over-rides all other obligations
they might have felt towards their fellow creatures,
although tradition may demand

conventional expressions of regret
at poisoned lakes and ravaged countryside:
'*the price we sadly pay for human Progress*',
or pious affirmations of goodwill
toward the poor they've ruined through their
structural economic readjustments
(or some such dismal claptrap).
The second form of human aberration,
the twin infection that has typified and marred the breed,
is violence, not through sly financiers'
hidden exercise of power,
but with brutal weapons and with rancid minds.

The lens that views these happenings
makes very clear that they are only
pustules in an off-shoot of the mind;
the area that harbours
illusions of reality that generate
the dubious business methods,
the coldness and the cruelty
of social systems and economies,
enslavement and colonialism,
raging dreams of military glory,
oppressive laws that, favouring the rich
deplete the poor, the clever bombs,
the planes that carry them, the inter-
continental missiles, poison gas,
the busy torture chambers
and, before all else,
The Will And the Ability To Use And To Apply Them

in the underlying faith that, being there, they may perhaps bring
happiness.

Meanwhile the real business of humanity
is stalled, and so delays
the drafting of just laws,
rejection of all weapons,
and generosity in love.

But the message is quite clearly sent around
by all the teachers:
To Honour Life You Must Disarm The Mind.

Now, somewhat paradoxically, it's true
that mind, the mind we must disarm,
the mind that's *mined* – excuse the pun –
that spawns the wounding weapons
and policies of harm and hatred
is also of the All, the Void, the very Everything;
how can this be,
this enigmatic contradiction?

The answer is, we know enough to think
we know it all.
The most of us will not wait quietly
for wisdom to sink in, but rush ahead
in ignorant omniscience,
filling the vacuum with proud,
self-serving drivel.

In this louche atmosphere
illusions spread like weeds:
that happiness is having,
that health is wealth,
that peace comes best through violence and victory
(and that this is proved by history)
that Ego's the king of the castle
and you're the shit in the arse hole.
And much more besides – feel free
to make up your own personalised illusion,
everyone else does.

Great cultures of the past, not always
good, but skilled and powerful,
have been built upon the flimsy
structure of such fantasies
and have collapsed, being just froth and foam,
because the wisdom of the few
and ever presence of the Mind's true majesty
blew upon and burst the empty bubbles.

So we must discover how to recognise
and then up-root the weapons in the mind:
the hates and irritations, fears and cravings
for petty things that change to monstrous lusts
that mobilise the hates, stir mobs to kill,
and blight the tender flowers of compassion.

Now how to solve the problem; there's the rub.
The key is to abandon judgement, not perfect it.
Our lives are full of judgements;
of assessment and comparison, brighter, dimmer,
more virtuous or less; applied to individuals,
to nations and to races; to morals and behaviour,
to religious creeds and to philosophies.
The basis always swivels round to me.

I or my teachers – my parents, my gurus
or my professors, my nation or my party,
whom I include within my wider self,
pronounce, even quite unconsciously,
judgement: this or that is better than
the other – which also means that I am
(or the country that I fight for).
These judgements spoil relations with the other.

Our distastes and preferences turn this or they
or that or those into crude parodies:
all Muslims are fanatic terrorists,
and Christians fat unscrupulous oppressors;
'*Them Frogs is proper bastards,
always have been since we was fighting them
with bows and arrows.*'
Small wonder that the French won't buy our beef!

And thus throughout our lives,
throughout our civilisations, we have stamped
the stain of self and judgement,
even on the ones we love the most –
perhaps them more than any,
and they inevitably pass it on.

Thus we have armed ourselves and others
against the enemies of ego.

How to disarm ourselves?
Again it's simple, but perversely hard:

to understand what's happening
and to remain awake against
the sleep of self and custom.

Then shall the weapons of destruction fall
unnoticed from our mental hands,
and the grace of individual lives
merge within the glory of the All.

Also published by Jon Carpenter

To Tame the Hydra

Undermining the culture of violence

Adam Curle

Curle likens the culture of violence to the mythical monster, the Hydra. Almost impossible to destroy, as soon as one vicious head is cut off, another grows.

The modern Hydra grows out of the morass of global economic and political interdependency where governments and businesses alike share a single common purpose: the pursuit of profit and power.

The gaps between the rich and the poor, the weak and the powerful, grow ever wider while threats of violence, environmental destruction and economic collapse are increasingly real. At the same time we experience a loss of happiness that has been falsely built on expectations of the fruits of wealth.

It is impossible to search meaningfully for 'peace' in the modern world unless we take on board—and combat—this contemporary Hydra.

Adam Curle examines how our very involvement in the Hydra of the modern economy makes it very difficult for us to destroy it. Yet he draws hope from experiences in Eastern Europe and South Africa, where real cultural change has followed a realisation among ordinary people of what is actually going on.

A book full of wit and wisdom.

£10 pbk   112pp   1 897766 51 3

To order, please phone 01689 870437 during office hours, or send a cheque for £10 to Jon Carpenter Publishing, Evenlode Books, Market Street, Charlbury OX7 3PH